The Relationship Roadmap
and Adventure Guide

Roger Crooks
MA, MSW, LCSW

ISBN 979-8-9927626-3-1 (Paperback)

Cover art by nskvsky
Book design by Taylor Crooks

Printed by IngramSpark in the United States of America.

First printing edition 2026.

Published by Bookcomber Publishing
rogercrooksjr@gmail.com

To Jolene,
The moment I met you I knew a wonderful
adventure had begun that would never end.

Table of Contents

Part 3: The Relationship Roadmap Adventure Guide

Part 4: The Relationship Roadmap 250+ Date Ideas and Score

Part 5: Relationship Extras, Challenges, Mantras, Surveys, and Checklists

Introduction

Welcome to *The Relationship Roadmap and Adventure Guide*! Most relationship books are overwhelming with lengthy case studies and technical psychobabble, but this book is radically different.

This book is full of hope and inspiration, spoken simply and honestly. It's absolutely jam-packed with adventure and new ways to nurture your relationship. It's short enough to be read in a day or two, but I hope you'll revisit the Adventure Guide part of the book for many years.

I've peppered inspirational quotes throughout the book. Please give extra attention to these nuggets of wisdom. At the end of each chapter, there is a mantra that summarizes the chapter and leaves you with a positive affirmation. There are also many activities with opportunities for you to enhance your relationship.

Relationships can be utterly hard, but they can also be a pinnacle of joy. When I read relationships books and articles in the past, I often looked for things that my partner needed to change. This was a mistake. As you read this book, I encourage you to think less about how your partner can change and more about how you can change! Your changes can initiate your partner's change. Improve yourself and the way you relate to your partner and your relationship will grow.

There is no one magic formula that can wow your partner and unlock their heart. Your partner is completely unique with their own set of needs, wants, and desires. You are also unique from every other human on Earth. You and your partner will come closer together with a formula that is as unique as you are. There are lots of ingredients in this book. Sample them until you find the perfect recipe for you.

You have the possibility to greatly improve your relationship and your life. It is my hope that you will learn how to be your partner's greatest lover and best friend. It's never too late to reclaim the love that you've always dreamed of and embrace a togetherful future.

A Message For the Skeptical Partner

So, your partner bought a relationship book. What does this mean? Could it mean your relationship is in crisis? Perhaps they are disappointed and dissatisfied? What it really means is that your partner loves you! They adore you so much that they want to build on the already great relationship you have and make it even better! While some people turn to addictions, pornography, or affairs, your partner is reinvesting in you!

How you react to this new challenge is up to you. You can laugh it off, get upset, or simply ignore it, but there is a much better response. Be willing to get on board and see where *The Relationship Roadmap* takes you. This book is full of rediscovery, fun, and adventures! I was once a hesitant skeptic too, but once I became more malleable, my life changed forever.

If you don't read the book, I hope that you'll honor your partner and try a few of the exercises and adventures they might propose to you. Take part in some new date night ideas. You really have nothing to lose and perhaps a much more enjoyable relationship to gain!

A Message For the Enthusiastic Partner

If you are the enthusiastic partner, it's likely you were the one who found this book. Good for you! Your partner may have no desire to join you in this quest for a better relationship. They may be perfectly content with how things are. I know this may be hard to accept, but hope is not lost.

You can improve your relationship with the ideas and activities in this book, even without your partner's participation. In fact, you might want to use some of the techniques in the book without ever telling your partner. That's okay too.

I've found that the more you love your partner, the easier it is for your partner to love you back. It is my deepest desire that what you are about to read will lead to a mutually gratifying relationship.

My Story

My relationship started with optimism and excitement, but it was wounded, with some of our dreams shattered. Major mistakes and transgressions were made. It got so hard that we separated and finally divorced. It was a gloomy and stressful time for all involved. Trust was destroyed, dreams foiled. Words really can't describe that type of heartache. I have overwhelming empathy for anyone who's been through this experience.

We often avoid talking about those dark times. There is still pain in thinking of those experiences, and sometimes the past is best left alone. As painful as it is to talk about the past, I understand that my past might be your present. If you are currently dealing with overwhelming relationship struggles, I hope that this book will give you hope and courage. You are not alone!

So, what happened that allowed us to come back from divorce and rekindle our fractured relationship? We softened our hearts, and we each had experiences that helped us turn to each other and give our failed relationship a second chance.

We grew a relationship that is infinitely better than either of us could have imagined. Old habits were broken and new traditions were made. Selfishness became selflessness. Joy in each day together became the new norm. We became a new couple.

How could two people overcome such incredible odds to redesign a failed relationship into one of hope, joy, and excitement? We've been asked this question by countless people who think our story is something special.

In the following pages, you'll find some of the secrets we discovered. It is my hope that by sharing my story, I can help increase the goodness and quality in your relationships.

If you are not already with your forever love, I hope that what I share will assist you in your future relationship. Knowing what you want upfront is a great way to set your standards high and not settle for less than what you deserve.

Part 1
The Relationship Roadmap Topics

Chapter 1
Expectations and Investments

"Building and repairing relationships
are long-term investments."

—*Stephen Covey*

Growing up, most of us have an idea of what our future partner will be like. Perhaps you dreamed of having that special person lifting you off your feet and tossing you through a whimsical life. I know I did.

The Problem with Expectations

We all have expectations of our partners. There are two major problems that come with these expectations:

- We expect things to be perfect, the way we dream them to be.
- We forget that the other person has expectations of us too.

When I met Jolene, I was swept away by her smile, and I knew she was the perfect package I had always dreamed of. After the "honeymoon" period wore off, I recognized areas where she didn't meet my ideal. Looking back, I realize I wasn't meeting her ideal either. We were unknowingly disappointing each other.

I wanted her to be the perfect girl of my dreams, but I wasn't giving her time to understand what that looked like. She couldn't possibly know all the things I desired. It was unfair of me to expect this. I never thought to ask her what the guy of her dreams was like either, I was oblivious of her desires.

Even when a partner gets close to perfection, we often push them so hard that it causes other problems. We exhaust them until they refuse to move any further in our direction. Nagging someone rarely produces the desired outcome. When a person acts out of obligation, both partners will be unsatisfied, and the relationship will suffer.

It is fine to encourage and educate someone to more perfectly love you, but it has to be done with patience, offering ample grace. Don't force someone to become something that they are not. That being said, we should willingly make adjustments to bring greater joy to our partner.

Recognizing Your Partner's Individuality

Sometimes I think we forget that our partners are separate and distinct from us. They have their own goals each day and plans for life. While these goals may include their partner, sometimes they won't. We must respect that our partner is unique and not responsible for our happiness.

**While your partner may add great joy to your life,
your individual happiness depends solely on you.**

Over many years, we have learned how to be more of each other's "ideal." We've adjusted because we see the happiness it brings the other when we align with their heartfelt desires. I believe we have both lowered our expectations to be more attainable for each other. We also show much more grace for each other's shortcomings. We all need grace.

Your Way, My Way... Our Way

We all have unique ways of doing things. Diversity in our daily lives is fine, but what do we do when our routine clashes with our partner's? I am a morning person. I forget what my morning alarm sounds like because I'm usually awake long before it goes off. Jolene, on the other hand, is a night person. The snooze button is a good friend of hers.

Early in our relationship, this contrast caused difficulties. I'd be ready to go in the early morning while she slept, and she'd be raring to go at night when I was exhausted! In those early days, I was sure that my way of living was the best way. I assumed morning people were healthy, wealthy, and wise! I'm sure Jolene thought otherwise. Who was right? The truth I understand now is that:

**Neither partner has a claim on the ultimate way to live life.
There is value in both partners' preferences.**

It took patience and grace to bridge our differences. Now, Jolene will lovingly wake up early when I have something special planned. Likewise, I'll stay up late for the events she wants me to attend. Otherwise, we embrace our differences and accept that I'll be up early and she'll be up late. This is only a problem if we make it one. We used to make it a problem, but we have matured. While we each hold fast to our unique ways of living life, we have learned to appreciate our differences. Instead of dividing us, it strengthens us. Differences are not right or wrong; they are simply preferences.

My Partner: An Important Part of My World

By all accounts, your partner should be the most important person in your world. You've committed to them, and you have plans to go the distance of life alongside each other. After mustering the courage to ask Jolene out on our first date, I designed it to be a fun group date. I invited many friends to join us on a trip to Price Park in the mountains of North Carolina for a picnic and to play kickball.

To get to know her better, I devised a simple game. Before the date, I had all the attendees fill out a questionnaire about themselves with fun and lighthearted questions. Without revealing their names, I randomly read the cards, and we all voted on who we thought the mystery person was based on their answers. There were about twelve of us there, and everyone said this game was their favorite part of the date. Months later, Jolene revealed that while watching me lead that game, she said to herself, "There is something special about this guy!"

How We Dated Then Versus How We Date Now

During those first magical weeks and months of a new relationship, we generally give everything we have to impress and nurture our new love. When we first started dating, Jolene valued every minute she could spend with me. I remember being beyond exhausted due to work and school responsibilities, but she craved my attention, and I gave it to her.

Do we change how we treat each other after we've been in a relationship for a while? I believe most of us do. We tend to lose some of that enchantment. We don't work as hard to impress our partner. This can be a letdown for either partner who thought it would always be magical and exciting.

Oh Those Dating Days!

For this activity, think back on your dating days. What did you enjoy about those first days, weeks, and months that you dated?

Partner #1 _____

Why I Chose You as My Partner:

Things I Loved About Our Dating & Courtship:

Things From Our Dating & Courtship I Wish We Could Do More:

Partner #2 _____

Why I Chose You as My Partner:

Things I Loved About Our Dating & Courtship:

Things From Our Dating & Courtship I Wish We Could Do More:

After reviewing the items your partner loved about your dating days, do you see any areas where you have changed? Could you reclaim some of that early relationship fun? I challenge you to choose something from your partner's list and do it together.

Cheerleading: A Key to Lifelong Love

In talking with couples who have grown a lifelong love, most share some similarities and habits. One habit is to become your partner's biggest cheerleader. We all love it when someone takes pride in our growth and achievements. It feels good to have someone show genuine interest in our accomplishments. We should all strive to be our partner's "go-to" when they have positive news to share. In times when our partners have self-doubt, it's even more important to cheer for them. We all need to be encouraged and lifted up from time to time.

Here are a few practical ways to cheer for your partner:

- **Celebratory Dinners**: Take your partner to a special restaurant to honor and treat them when they have something to celebrate.
- **Greeting Cards**: Provide a card that expresses pride in your partner. This can be given, mailed, or even hidden for them to find.
- **Phone and Text**: Contact someone who has a mutual interest in your partner's accomplishments and share noteworthy news. Brag about your partner when they can hear you and also declare their accomplishments when they aren't around.
- **Social Media Acknowledgment**: Few of us are outgoing enough to brag about our own accomplishments, so consider giving your partner a shout-out!

Years ago, I visited the home of a man who had lost the love of his life. They had been married for over fifty years. As I talked with him, he shared how special his wife was and how skilled she was at noticing small details. She once caught a bank's error in the amount of one penny.

Joyously, he showed me a framed check from the bank for one cent. He had framed it for her as a gift. Even after her death, he remained her biggest cheerleader, telling stories about how special she was. It thrills me to hear couples cheer for and brag about each other.

And Yet I'm Still Loved

I have said some really dumb things throughout my life with Jolene. Nevertheless, she looks past my foot-in-the-mouth moments and loves me anyway. We have also said hurtful things to each other, things I know we both wish we could take back. We will probably never forget some of the words that have hurt us, but:

Forgiving isn't forgetting.
Forgiving is remembering with grace, love, and gentleness.

I've done some immature things, as most of us have. We can't change anything that's happened; the past is set. How awesome is it to have a partner who can overlook and forgive our missteps? Looking past each other's imperfections with a forgiving heart is incredibly special. I appreciate it when people show me grace for my past words and deeds. Life is too short to hold grudges or continually bring up the painful past to those around us.

Forgiving Yourself

Perhaps harder than forgiving others is learning to forgive yourself. I have wasted a lot of time wallowing in sorrow over poor choices. I know that many others needlessly suffer for their past mistakes. I am guilty of using negative self-talk, thinking things like: "If I could just go back in time," "I really screwed up my life," or "I hate what I have done."

Recently, while driving, I started this same nagging, negative thinking. I paused and had another thought: Maybe I didn't screw up. Maybe I learned a valuable lesson. Yes! I felt a slight decrease in negativity, and then I said it out loud: "I have learned so much over my life!"

Your mistakes are in the past, but fortunately, you get to take the hard
lessons learned with you into the future.

You may never feel perfectly "whole" as you reflect on your life choices, but the consequence of those choices is knowledge. Use that knowledge to guide you to a better future. You didn't just mess up; you grew.

Revealing Your True Self

Most of us hide our thoughts and feelings from others. We can be very guarded about what we do and don't share. Joseph Luft and Harry Ingham introduced the concept of the Johari Window to describe how we directly and indirectly reveal ourselves to others and how others view us.

Essentially, we all have things we know about ourselves that no one else does (our private thoughts and experiences). There are also things we reveal to others (our public persona). Third, there are things others know about us that we are unaware of (our blind spots). Finally, there are things about us that are unknown to both us and others (deep-seated truths about ourselves). The Johari Window has four "window panes," and these can vary in size. This idea has resonated with me for many years.

Using the ideas of the Johari Window, I believe that when we are alone with our partners, we aren't really alone. There are multiple versions of ourselves present, including how we see ourselves, how we see each other, and the elusive version of who we truly are. This doesn't mean we are purposely deceptive with our partners; we just can't see all the angles of our identity or why we do some of the things we do.

Close partners will open up about things they would keep hidden from everyone else, expanding the "revealing to others" window pane. How open are you with your partner? Consider how much you keep hidden and evaluate whether you should reveal more or less of your hidden self.

Our partners can become confidants for our secret thoughts, experiences, and desires. They can also become keenly aware of our weaknesses and fears.

Jolene knows things about me that no one else does. I have been reluctant to share some of my hidden self with her. Fortunately, she welcomes my disclosures, and she shares things with me too. It is so special to have someone to reveal your true self to—flaws and all—and still be loved by them. This doesn't mean everything needs to be revealed, but it is refreshing to have someone you can be yourself with.

Three's Company

Many couples have had a third party enter all aspects of their relationship. No, I'm not referring to Mr. Roper, the cranky and hilarious landlord from *Three's Company*. I'm referring to the smartphone, that wonderful and pesky tool that nestles its way into romantic dinners, date nights, and even the bedroom! Some of you may not mind this third party as part of your intimate relationship, but it's something I don't want in mine. Don't misunderstand me; I enjoy the smartphone and the wondrous things it can do. I just don't like how it can absorb time and attention from relationships. Time is everything.

**"Time is the most precious commodity that's out there.
It's the one thing that you can't buy or ever buy back."**
—*Jaret Grossman*

Before the smartphone invasion, more couples spent the final moments of the day in bed talking, snuggling, and loving each other. I have a personal rule: I don't look at or touch my phone when I'm in bed.

This way, my mind can slow down, and I can give precious attention to my partner. I encourage you to try breaking the cycle of smartphone and social media addiction. For millennia, humans went to bed without a phone in hand, and we can too. Give it a try. There's a great chance you'll bond more with your partner and sleep better too.

Mantra:

We have a rich history together. Of all the people we could be with, we chose each other. My partner is an important part of my world.

Chapter 2
We ALL have a Past

"Every long lost dream led me to where you are. Others who broke my heart they were like northern stars pointing me on my way into your loving arms. This much I know is true that God blessed the broken road that led me straight to you."

—*Rascal Flatts, Bless The Broken Road*

We must understand that we all have a past. Every emotional, physical, and sexual relationship we've had has changed us in some way. More often than not, we are unaware of the full impact that past relationships have on us in the present.

From early childhood, we learn unique sets of rules, norms, and guidelines from those around us. Parental influences can go so far back that we may not remember when we were imprinted with them. Many of the relational rules we live by today may have been established in years or experiences we don't even recall.

Sadly, many of us have also been victims of trauma. Some of these experiences can be horrific, such as physical, verbal, emotional, or sexual abuse. Less traumatic events may also be problematic and remain stuck in our memories.

Our past relationships also shape how we interpret the present. How we were treated, both positively and negatively, can create unwritten rules and expectations. Grievous treatment, such as rape or coerced sex, can leave lifelong scars and significantly impact every relationship that follows.

None of us enter a permanent relationship without imperfections and faulty ways of thinking. If traumatic events occurred when we were very young, it can be difficult to pinpoint their origins. Sometimes something as subtle as the smell of passing perfume or cologne or a familiar song can trigger memories buried deep within us and evoke powerful emotions. The good news is that we do not need to be bound by our past. We can overcome it.

While we are helpless to change the past, we decide our present each day. We are the architects of our future.

Your trauma is not your fault! Sometimes professional help is necessary. Several times in this book, I'll recommend seeking outside help. In each of these situations, I suggest finding a doctor, therapist, or counselor to help you overcome your challenges. When seeking a professional, be careful about whom you entrust with your body, mind, and heart. Be selective. If things are not improving, consider finding a new provider. Support groups and other community resources can also assist with a variety of issues.

Healing Wounds and Rewriting the Past

If you've experienced trauma that isn't severe enough to require therapy, you may be able to heal on your own. You can relearn and readjust your mind by adopting new ways to think about your struggles. One effective method is to rewrite the past.

Transform your troubles by thinking differently about them. Here's a simple example of rewriting the past:

Imagine your partner loves lying on the beach in the middle of the day and wants you to join them. Typically, this is when the beach is hot and crowded. You don't want to sit on a hot, crowded beach—you've always hated them! If you dwell on the negatives and anticipate a terrible day, it will likely be a miserable experience.

However, if you challenge yourself to think positively, you can enjoy the day. Start by recognizing that your partner appreciates your company. Then, look around the beach: Are there things that could make the day not only bearable but enjoyable? Notice how the warm sand feels under your feet. Perhaps you'll enjoy people-watching. As you sit, you might realize it's not as hot as you expected, or the beach isn't as crowded as you thought. Before long, you may find yourself enjoying that warm beach day!

You're unlikely to feel as miserable in the future because you've retrained your brain to be okay with hot beaches. You may not love hot, crowded beaches, but you've shown yourself you can handle them and even find joy in them.

> ### "There ain't no future in the past."
> ### —*Vince Gill*

By rewriting past situations, you can transform your emotions and experiences. This technique works! Start by practicing with small annoyances, like a hot beach day, and soon you'll be able to reframe past struggles into strengths. Let's consider a more traumatic experience to see how this method can help.

Imagine you went to the movies as a teen and were aggressively groped and sexually exploited by a date. Naturally, you might avoid dark movie theaters with your current partner. To rewrite this uncomfortable memory, challenge yourself to attend a movie and aim for a better experience. The respect your current partner shows you can help calm your nerves. As you focus on enjoying the movie, your anxiety may lessen. After a positive experience, attending movies with your partner will likely become easier. By rewriting this memory, you'll reclaim a small part of your past.

Rewriting traumatic events can free you and your current partner from negative patterns reinforced over the years. I've used this technique to address my own trauma with great success. I know it's not easy to revisit a place tied to trauma, but try to stay in that uncomfortable moment and allow yourself to relax. Real progress comes as you reframe past missteps and negative experiences to reclaim your past.

Time, The Great Healer

My first solo bike ride ended in a disastrous wreck. I scratched up my arms, face, and legs. That was decades ago, and the miracle of the human body has healed those physical wounds. Emotional wounds can also heal or improve with time. Be patient with yourself and your partner as you progress slowly. Trust in the healing power of time. Some past wounds may never fully heal, and that's not necessarily a bad thing.

Remembering painful events can help us avoid repeating the same mistakes. However, rumination—constantly replaying a painful event—does no good. It's easier said than done, but we should avoid beating ourselves up over past poor choices, whether our own or our partner's. Rumination doesn't improve the present; it only derails our hopes for a brighter future. Confront your rumination head-on!

When struggling with rumination, ask yourself two questions:
- "Can I change what I'm thinking about?"
- "Will worrying change anything?"

If you can't change it, say to yourself, "Enjoy today!" Another strategy I've found helpful is to assign a specific day and time for rumination—for me, it's Tuesday mornings. When you start ruminating outside that time, remind yourself it's not your scheduled moment and let the thought go. This works because you're taking control of the rumination, making it less powerful. Like all coping strategies, this requires practice. Don't give up without giving it time to work. I know from experience how hard it is to stop dwelling on the past. With small steps, you can do it!

Unfortunate Jealousy

At some point, we all feel jealousy. Jolene once shared a story about a date with an old boyfriend. Although it was an innocent tale about a haunted house, I felt jealous that her fun memory didn't involve me. Conversely, I once told her about a date I had. One night out with our friends, she shared my story with them, finding it hilarious enough to recount. Unlike me, Jolene showed no jealousy about my story. Clearly, she demonstrated greater emotional maturity than I did.

Jealousy often stems from fragile egos and self-doubt. Ego is one of humanity's biggest shortcomings. Ryan Holiday's book, *Ego Is the Enemy*, captures this idea perfectly. Recognizing that your partner may struggle with insecurity can help you respond with compassion when they feel jealous.

> **"Ego is the enemy."**
> —*Ryan Holiday*

If you're the jealous partner, reflect on why you feel self-doubt. Why do you compare yourself to others? What is the underlying insecurity? Find ways to build confidence in who you are. You'll never win by comparing yourself to others. Your partner is with you now; you have their heart. You've won!

> **"Intense jealousy telegraphs intense insecurity."**
> —*Zachary Stockill*

Couples who share too much about past relationships risk a slippery slope, often ending like my ill-fated childhood bike ride. While some details should be disclosed, others can cause more harm than good.

Walking With Your Partner Through Jealousy

When your partner struggles with jealousy and self-doubt, you can help them feel more secure. Here are three strategies I propose:

1. **Affirm their strengths**. Highlight what you love and adore about them. Boost their confidence in areas where they feel insecure. It's hard to stay jealous when your partner's genuine praise lifts your spirits.

2. **Be transparent**. Reduce jealousy by being open. Share your passwords and location with your partner to show you have nothing to hide. This builds trust and reassures them of your commitment.

3. **Address the root of their jealousy**. Identify why your partner feels jealous and focus on those areas. Some common reasons for jealousy include:

   - Past betrayals. Previous experiences of infidelity or broken trust.
   - Unmet needs. Your partner may feel their needs are not being met.
   - Low self-esteem. They may feel unworthy or compare themselves to others.
   - Fear of loss. Anxiety about losing you to someone else can fuel jealousy.
   - Lack of communication. Misunderstandings or unclear intentions may spark insecurity.
   - Perceived favoritism. Your partner may think you prioritize others' needs over theirs.
   - Glamorizing your past. They may assume you loved others more than you love them.

Some people may remain jealous even when you do everything right. In these cases, express your love, show grace, and let time work its magic. Revisit my three strategies to guide them through their jealousy, but ultimately, the burden is theirs to overcome.

Welcome to My Past!

During this activity, think about the times that you wish your partner could have been with you from your past. Are there certain moments you would have wanted their company or support? Are there special moments you've always wished they could have enjoyed with you?

Partner #1 _____

What moments from your past do you wish your partner could have been with you?

-
-
-

What moment or moments of your partner's past do you wish you could have participated in and been a part of?

-
-
-

Partner #2 _____

What moments from your past do you wish your partner could have been with you?

-
-
-

What moment or moments of your partner's past do you wish you could have participated in and been a part of?

-
-
-

Mantra:

We come from different backgrounds with unique experiences. The individual choices we made led us to each other. Together we will create a beautiful path into the future.

Chapter 3
Communication

"Communication is the mortar that
holds a relationship together."
—*Amy Bellows*

In conversations, we sometimes focus too much on our own responses instead of truly listening. Active listening should be every couple's goal. Avoid formulating a response until you fully understand your partner's message. Inattentive listening signals a lack of care. Many couples find it harder to communicate with each other than with people outside the relationship, often being more critical of their partner and offering less grace than they do others.

Withhold judgment when your partner shares their thoughts. Jumping to conclusions without letting them fully express themselves hinders communication. Being defensive further complicates matters.

Everything we hear is filtered through our personal perspectives, which can distort our partner's intended meaning. If only we could clearly understand each other's true intentions! Reformulating what your partner says in a positive way allows you to respond constructively, strengthening the relationship.

Here are two examples:

1. Request to Clean the Kitchen
   - Scenario: One partner asks the other to clean the kitchen, even though it's not typically their responsibility.
   - Negative Interpretation and Response: "Really? I work all day, and this is what I come home to?"
   - Positive Interpretation and Response: "I'm not a fan of cleaning the kitchen, but I'm a fan of you, so I'll make this kitchen sparkle!"

2. Request for More Intimacy
   - Scenario: One partner expresses that there hasn't been enough intimacy in the relationship over the past few weeks.
   - Negative Interpretation and Response: "Oh my gosh, I can't believe you're bringing this up again. You frustrate me so much!"
   - Positive Interpretation and Response: "You're the sweetest! I've never been adored like this, and I love that you can't get enough of me. I love you so much!"

Can you see how a simple shift in thinking can transform your emotions? This is the core of Rational Emotive Behavior Therapy (REBT): our thoughts shape our emotions, so changing how we think changes how we feel. Can we be mature enough to recognize the positive intentions behind our partner's words? Positive interpretation is a powerful approach that can dramatically strengthen your relationship. How couples receive critique determines whether they argue or grow closer. Positively reframing interpretations and responses is one of the most impactful strategies in this book. Practice this approach often, and it can transform your life!

False Assumptions

We all make assumptions about others daily, and often, these assumptions are wrong. Years ago, a relative mentioned she enjoyed lighthouses. Attentive listeners took this to mean she loved lighthouses! For years, she received lighthouse-themed gifts, framed prints, ceramics, and nautical novelties. We were surprised when she later casually admitted she didn't actually like lighthouses all that much. Our well-meaning but false assumption led to years of misguided gift-giving. We appreciated her honesty, and now we only gift her lighthouse tchotchkes as a joke.

> "Assumptions are the termites of relationships."
> —*Henry Winkler*

Jolene and I have made many false assumptions throughout our relationship, causing both minor and significant damage. We've worked to clear up most of these misinterpretations, but it remains an ongoing challenge.

Attentive Listening

Most of us love talking about ourselves and our passions. It doesn't take much to encourage someone to open up if you give them the opportunity. My uncles, Tim and Rich, are experts at this. They showed genuine interest in my autographed trading card collection, allowing me to share my passion joyfully. By listening intently, they make everyone feel special. I encourage us all to follow their example by treating our partners with the same attentiveness.

Listen closely to your partner. If you're a big talker, dial it back to let them participate. Your moments of silence may be just what they need to open up.

You'll be amazed at how much you learn by listening and showing interest. Listening is love.

While shopping with Jolene for jewelry, we played a fun game where I guessed which pieces she liked. I listened carefully as she explained what was special about each one, learning her preferences for colors, shapes, and materials. Now, I'm far better prepared to surprise her with gifts she'll love. Being attentive to your partner can greatly strengthen your relationship.

Attentive Listening with Clarification

After listening intently, ensure your interpretation is accurate. Ask clarifying questions to confirm you understand your partner's message. Jolene, a sign language interpreter for most of her life, knows this well. When interpreting ASL to English, errors can easily occur. Professional interpreters are trained to seek clarification when unsure about a message. To ensure you grasp what your partner is expressing, follow their example by asking for clarification as needed. This can be as simple as saying, "So, what I think you're saying is…" This practice strengthens communication and deepens your connection.

Writing Scripts

"Don't write scripts!" is a well-known saying in our household. A script is a preconceived notion about a person's thoughts or intentions—an assumption taken to the next level that may or may not be true. Assigning words or thoughts to your partner that they may not even hold is unfair. I'm guilty of this relationship mistake, and I suspect I'm not alone.

Consider this scenario: "Change of plans, we won't eat out tonight; I'll make dinner."

A scriptwriter might respond, "That cheapskate knows we don't have anything planned for dinner. He'd better not make ramen again!"

Little did they know, steaks were on sale, and the plan was to grill at home.

Scriptwriting is especially common in texting, where messages can be interpreted in countless ways. Without visual cues, texts are easily misunderstood, particularly by a scriptwriter. Avoid texting emotionally charged conversations, as raw text lacks tone and context, often leading to misinterpretation. I've lost count of how many times Jolene and I have misunderstood a text, sometimes with unfortunate consequences.

Unwavering Honesty

Lies and dishonesty can devastate a relationship. Strive to build bonds of honesty and integrity in communication with your partner. Telling the whole truth is not only essential but also deeply endearing.

"If you tell the truth, you don't have to remember anything."
—Mark Twain

When your partner shares something difficult, acknowledge their honesty and ask for time to process before responding. Avoiding a knee-jerk reaction fosters more positive outcomes. To encourage ongoing honesty and transparency, respond maturely to their revelations. If you react with anger or become upset, your partner may hesitate to be truthful in the future.

Undivided Attention

Technology has made it harder to give someone our full attention. In the past, a daily newspaper might have distracted couples, but today's electronic devices are far more disruptive.

My advice? Put the phone away when communicating with your partner. No one enjoys sitting across from someone glued to their screen, responding to every notification. This applies to other distractions, too—books, television, music. Ignore them to avoid missing a crucial moment in the conversation.

I struggle most at restaurants, where televisions on the walls draw my eyes, even when nothing interesting is playing. I've learned to sit with my back to screens and made a pact to never use my phone during the restaurant experience. Devote your full attention to your partner to strengthen your connection.

"Love begins with listening."
—Mr. Rogers

In a world where your partner rarely receives full attention, you can be the one person they trust to share their experiences, thoughts, and feelings completely. By focusing intently on their every word, noticing nonverbal cues, and looking into their eyes with genuine interest, you love them in a rare and special way. This kind of attention stands out. Your partner will know you're the person they can always turn to when they feel ignored or neglected by others. They'll confide in you. In a world full of distractions, be their anchor of attentiveness.

A Listening Ear or an Advisor?

For years, Jolene shared her personal struggles with me, and I eagerly offered my thoughts, even when she didn't ask for them. Though I meant to help, my advice didn't always comfort her. It took me a long time to realize she often just needed a listening ear. When your partner shares their burdens, lovingly ask:

"Do you want me to listen, or do you want my advice?"

This question lets your partner guide the response they need, helping you serve each other better. Remember, listening is love.

When to Ask For More or Different Things

Sometimes, we may want something more or different from our partner. If you're unhappy with an aspect of your relationship, when's the best time to discuss it? I'm about to share one of the most valuable pieces of relationship advice I know. It's so simple that many experts overlook it, and most people don't even consider it. Here it is:

Ask for more of what you want from your partner when things are going well!

That's the big secret! The ideal time to request change is when your relationship is thriving. Asking during a struggle often worsens the situation, leaving your request unmet.

Request, Don't Demand

How you express your desires matters. Kind requests are far better received than snarky demands. Consider this example:

Snarky Demand: "You haven't taken me out to eat all week. The least you could do is get groceries."

This triggers defensiveness and resentment. Contrast it with:

Kind Request: "The only thing that could make me happier is a nice meal out with you."

This request is far more likely to be considered because it's presented lovingly. Positive communication fosters positive outcomes.

The 30 Minute Reunion Rule

Agree together that the first 30 minutes you reconnect after work (or a long day apart) should be exclusively positive. Greet each other with a warm smile and perhaps even a loving moment of physical connection. Make it a priority to use only optimistic and uplifting language, sharing only good news.

Too often, couples unintentionally drown each other with complaints, stresses, and everything that went wrong. These toxic reunions lead to emotional withdrawal, avoidance, and perhaps even dread.

Committing to the 30 Minute Reunion Rule creates a buffer against stress spillover and strengthens emotional connection. When I instituted this rule in my relationship, I went from feeling neutral about coming home to becoming excited to reconnect!

Valiantly Validate

To conclude this chapter, I want to emphasize the importance of validation in relationships. This is something I still struggle with. During arguments, Jolene often asks, "Do you see my point?" or "Do you really hear me?" It took me a long time to realize she wasn't trying to win arguments—she just wanted to know her opinions and feelings mattered.

Validate your partner by acknowledging their perspective. Here's a newsflash: you aren't always right. Both viewpoints usually have merit. Try these sentence starters to validate your partner:

- "I hear what you're saying and until you said that I didn't even realize..."
- "Your perspective makes sense to me."

- "I appreciate you sharing that. It helps me see where you're coming from."
- "I can see why this matters to you, and I value your thoughts."

Validation isn't a magic wand, but it's a very powerful tool. When you validate your partner's perspective, you may come to appreciate their viewpoint, soften your stance, and perhaps even agree with them. Many disagreements are trivial in the grand scheme of things. For example, I initially disliked the lamps Jolene once sent me photos of, but after validating her enthusiasm, I softened my heart and grew to love them. Validation shows your partner their voice matters, strengthening your bond.

Chapter 4
Problem Solving for Solutions

$\sim$

"Problems are only opportunies with thorns in them."
—Hugh Miller

Planning ahead is the best way to avoid major disputes. It keeps couples focused rather than frustrated. What are your goals for home, employment, family size, and other major life decisions? Discuss these early in a relationship. Unfortunately, love's initial thrill often blinds us, making these topics seem less important than attraction.

Jolene makes big decisions quickly, while I analyze everything. For purchases over $20, I consult *Consumer Reports* and read multiple reviews, taking a methodical approach Jolene might call rigid. She's spontaneous, which I might call haphazard. Thankfully, we've learned to appreciate each other's differences. Some decisions benefit from her quick action, while others require my careful consideration.

**When couples respect and adapt to each other's styles,
they gain the best of both worlds.**

Disagreements and stubbornness are inevitable, and it can be jarring to discover that the "perfect" person in your world holds different opinions. How do you navigate such contrasts? Start by valuing your partner's perspective and finding balance through open communication.

Learning to Let Go

Many problems can be resolved by letting go. Learning to be more laid-back when potential disagreements arise can prevent escalation, though this is challenging for those with controlling tendencies.

Jolene loves pillows—so many that we have more than places to put them! When our bed is made, the pillows cover half of it. This used to frustrate me as she constantly replaced and upgraded them. My loving teasing turned into irritation. One day, I realized how silly it was to fuss over something that brought her joy. Why make a big deal out of it? I was being immature. I decided to change my attitude. When Jolene proudly showed me two new pillows she "couldn't live without," I matched her excitement and exclaimed, "I love them!"

They were actually quite pretty. She was shocked by my change of heart, and we shared a unifying moment.

Since then, we've enjoyed looking at pillows together, and I even point out ones I like. If swapping pillows makes her happy, why not celebrate her purchases and grow closer rather than be a miserable grump? Fighting or obstructing our partner is a form of control, and controlling personalities can be hard to live with. Learn to let go of the need to control.

**It is often when we give up control of the wheel
that we enjoy the best ride of our life.**

How many disputes could you let go of? After my success with the pillows, I've tried releasing other small annoyances. To my surprise, "giving in" hasn't meant losing a battle—it's won me a happier partner, friend, and lover. One of the greatest pieces of relationship advice I can offer is to let go of the little things, and even many of the bigger ones.

Give Change a Try

As a Boy Scout, I loved camping, but now I have no desire to "rough it." Jolene, however, romanticizes camping and always wanted to buy an RV. I prefer rentals and hotels, and we've debated this for years. To humor her, I agreed to try an overnight RV stay during a vacation. To my surprise, she didn't enjoy it as much as she'd hoped. Her RV itch was scratched, and the debate faded. I didn't tell her, but the RV wasn't so bad.

Trial runs can reveal the pros and cons of ideas you disagree on. Be a good sport and try new things with an open mind, even admitting when you like your partner's suggestions. Jolene has proposed many home changes I initially resisted, but more often than not, I've come to love them. When your partner suggests a change, respond with an optimistic, "Let's go for it!" This openness strengthens your bond in indescribable ways.

Fun Ways to Resolve Small Conflicts

Rock, Paper, Scissors

- A fun way to settle minor disputes is Rock, Paper, Scissors. It's a quick, fair solution for deciding who cooks, takes out the trash, or handles other small tasks.

3, 2, 1…Go!

- Our favorite way to choose restaurants or date night locations is for one partner to suggest three places they'd enjoy. The other partner picks the final choice from those options, ensuring both have a say in the decision. Sometimes, we start with five choices and narrow it down to one. This method also works for decisions like selecting furniture or paint colors. I love how it encourages collaboration, bringing partners together to reach a shared decision.

Airing Grievances: A Warning

We've all seen couples air their grievances on social media. I feel very embarrassed for those who post angry rants about their partners online. This immature, toxic approach to conflict will never yield satisfying results.

> **"If you could kick the person responsible for most of your troubles, you wouldn't be able to sit down for six months."**
> —*Gordon Gray*

Confiding in someone about your struggles can be more productive—a close friend, loving family member, or counselor who can listen well. However, use them as a sounding board, not a coach. Don't rely solely on their opinions.

Your confidant cares about you and may instinctively side with you, which can create false beliefs about your situation. Getting hyped up by a friend might lead to poor decisions. You're responsible for your choices, so ensure they reflect your own judgment.

Times You Truly Disagree

Even with validation, perspective-taking, and letting go of small issues, large-scale disagreements can still arise. If you've practiced these skills—and aren't someone who disagrees just for the sake of it—resolving conflicts becomes easier. While I can't address every major disagreement, most can be resolved by truly listening to your partner's point of view, even when it seems incomprehensible. Be open to learning about their perspective.

Years ago, I learned a technique that fosters deep respect for your partner's viewpoint: argue for their side. Defending their position against your own is powerful. Try it during your next disagreement, it can open your eyes. Once you understand each other's perspectives, negotiating a solution that works for both becomes much easier. Aim for compromise, where both partners get some of what they want. Don't see it as "my way" or "your way," but as "our way." A win-win solution emerges when couples work together, and in most cases, they can agree on a shared path forward.

In relationships we shouldn't give in or give up, we should give love.

One of our most difficult conflicts is about where we will live. I'm comfortable in each home we have lived in while Jolene could move every year. In one heated battle over the home, I stated why we shouldn't move and Jolene shared why we should. To solve this, we compromised. She agreed to stay in the home and I agreed to make upgrades to the house. The bitter battle ended as a win- win as we enjoyed the updated house and added value to our home.

Arguing: Fast Track to Derail Progress

In a relationship, the best way to handle a fire is to avoid adding more fuel. Don't avoid uncomfortable communication, but be wise in how you respond. Sometimes it may be best to not respond at all.

> **"Among my prized possessions are
> words that I have never spoken."**
> *—Orson Scott Card*

I know when my comments might worsen a situation, so I resist the urge to prove a point. Working toward harmony in a relationship leads to better outcomes than insisting on "being right." When you argue or raise your voice to make a point, pause and reflect. At that moment, you are damaging the relationship. When my daughter, Taylor, was young, she struggled with not being right. Once, when I asked her to stop arguing, she said something so funny that I've never forgotten it.

> **"I'm not arguing, I'm clarifying that I'm right!"**
> *—Taylor Crooks*

Sometimes "being right" comes at a high cost. Arguing may feel satisfying in the moment, but it damages relationships and erodes respect. There are better alternatives to aggressively proving a point. Communicate calmly, seek common ground, show love, offer grace, and move forward with optimism.

Apology 101

When you have wronged your partner, you must apologize sincerely. When apologizing, avoid the word "but." Consider this apology with a "but":

"I'm sorry I didn't give you more attention at the party last night, but I was excited to catch up with old friends."

Contrast that with this apology:

"I'm truly sorry I didn't give you more attention at the party last night. I was thoughtless, and I'm committed to doing better."

Using "but" undermines the apology by turning it into an excuse. When you've wronged someone, there should be no "buts." Apologies are also meaningless without changed behavior. Acknowledge your mistakes, strive to avoid repeating them, and seek grace. Forgiveness and grace are precious gifts that should be offered and received.

It's Hard to Be You!

Although I don't know you, I'm certain life can be challenging for you! You handle so much. You're often so focused on meeting others' needs that you neglect your own. Life is also tough for your partner, who faces daily struggles and disappointments. We can get so caught up in our own world that we fail to recognize their challenges.

Jolene works from home all day while I work in an office. When I get home, I'm ready to relax, but she's eager to get out of the house. This caused tension between us until I spent a few days working from home and saw her perspective. I witnessed the demands she faced in her home office and realized I couldn't do her job. That experience helped me understand how she felt.

Developing the ability to see another's perspective is like receiving a map to avoid misunderstandings.

Life is hard, but that's why you and your partner should face each day together! Support each other, argue less, and find more ways to agree.

Mantra

While life can be hard, I will find success for myself and my relationship. We will overcome setbacks and find beautifully smooth solutions.

Chapter 5
Goals and Planning

"If you don't know where you are going,
you might wind up someplace else."
—*Yogi Berra*

The primary goal for many of us is simply to make it through the day. We've all been there. Without more meaningful goals, we wander aimlessly, like Alice in Wonderland.

> **Alice: Would you tell me, please, which way I ought to go from here?**
> **Cheshire Cat: That depends a good deal on where you want to get to.**
> **Alice: I don't much care where.**
> **Cheshire Cat: Then it doesn't matter which way you go.**
> —*Lewis Carroll, Alice in Wonderland*

Jolene is a goal-driven planner who meticulously keeps calendars, journals, and notebooks filled with plans and goals for our future. I sometimes cringe when she asks where I see myself in five years. When she inquires about my goals, I occasionally assume it's a trap to align me with her vision. However, instead of resisting her need to plan, I've found that embracing it is a more successful and enjoyable venture. When you align with your partner, you can both steer happily toward a shared future.

Discover Personal Goals

Personal goals are independent of our partner's goals. Being in a relationship shouldn't alter them. What are yours?

Partner #1 _____

Short Term Goals (1year):

Intermediate Term Goals (2-5 years):

Long Term Goals (5 or more years):

Partner #2 _____

Short Term Goals (1year):

Intermediate Term Goals (2-5 years):

Long Term Goals (5 or more years):

Discover Couple Goals

Couple goals should be created together with your partner. Identify goals you both share and include a few you haven't yet agreed on. In time, you may choose to pursue each other's goals. For now, prioritize the goals you both agree on.

Short Term Goals (1 year)

Intermediate Term Goals (2-5 years)

Long Term Goals (5 or more years)

We Have Goals, Now What?

One way to achieve your goals is by creating an action plan. An action plan breaks your goals into smaller, manageable steps. These checkpoints help you track your progress. Review your personal and couple goals, identify the steps needed to accomplish them, and work through them methodically. You've got this!

Flexibility and Alterations

When I was 20, I wrote five short-term, intermediate, and long-term goals for myself, putting careful thought into each of the fifteen goals. I'm proud of the ones I've achieved and at peace with those I haven't. My dreams have evolved since then. As situations and circumstances change, some goals need to be adjusted.

Be okay with change. Better yet, embrace it!

Life circumstances may alter some of your goals. Remember, you can always create new goals or update existing ones to better align with your current needs.

Mantra

I have goals that I will accomplish. As I pursue my own goals I will also encourage my partner in their goals. Together we will overcome all setbacks. We will accomplish our unified goals.

Chapter 6
Children and Family

~

"Family is the life jacket on the stormy sea of life."
—*J.K. Rowling*

We have rows of scrapbooks filled with memories of our children's early years. Children bring variety and vibrancy to life. Parenting comes with its own unique joys and challenges. "Family" remains one of my favorite words.

**Family encompasses all those whom we gather around us
with the most special of connections.**

Parenting

Children inevitably transform your relationship with your partner. Nearly all parents want their children to enjoy happy childhoods. To achieve this, you must strengthen your bond with your partner, as your relationship significantly shapes your children's lives.

**Children learn about future relationships by
observing the one they witness up close.**

In my work with teenagers, it's heartbreaking to see those caught in abusive relationships. Often, their parents experienced similar abuse. Could these teens be replicating the only relationship models they know? We should strive to model the healthy relationships we want our children to emulate. While children will ultimately choose their own paths, you can take pride in providing them with a blueprint for happiness.

Parenting as a Team

Disagreements over parenting can drive a wedge between partners. A unified, consistent approach to parenting is essential. Children need to view both parents as equals, not one as the disciplinarian and the other as a pushover. Discuss and agree with your partner on how to handle situations, and support each other consistently.

Parenting negotiations should take place privately, away from your children. You never know what they might overhear through walls or doors. Be mindful when discussing your children or parenting plans.

Weekly Family Night

In addition to scheduling date nights with your partner, set aside a weekly time for family. These moments should center on your children. Plan an activity to enjoy together, such as a board game night, an evening of bowling, or simply sharing your talents at home. I still cherish an old recording of a memorable talent show we held during one of our family nights when our children were young.

Enjoy All Phases of Parenting

Years ago, as I wrestled one of my children into a diaper, my grandfather watched my struggle. McKay, a rambunctious toddler, burst free from me, laughing. Exhausted, I jokingly complained to my grandfather. His face grew serious, and he said, "These are the best years of your life. When my boys were little, I didn't realize it was the happiest time of my life. Don't wish this time away."

His words carried a poignant mix of sadness and joy. From that moment, I never complained about a diaper again. I cherish my family deeply and have worked to build strong bonds with each of them. Here is a special message dedicated to my daughter, Taylor...

"Some people are worth melting for."
—*Olaf, Frozen*

In-laws

I was fortunate to have wonderful in-laws. My father-in-law, Jack, passed away shortly after our first child was born, but I grew very close to my mother-in-law, Elaine. I adore her and learned basic sign language to communicate with her more effectively. She is an angel. I also consider my brothers-in-law, Jon and Jarvis, as close friends. Not everyone enjoys an ideal in-law relationship. What do you do when things aren't smooth? My advice: give space, show grace, and then embrace.

Give Space

Being overly involved can strain your relationship with your in-laws. Give them opportunities for alone time with your partner. When in-laws don't feel they're competing for their adult child's attention, it can meet their needs and ease tensions. Aim for occasional, not unlimited, space. Balance is key.

Show Grace

In-laws are not perfect, and you shouldn't expect them to be. There are many reasons—some valid—why in-laws might struggle to accept their child's partner. For some parents, letting go of their child is difficult. Others may feel no one is ever good enough for their child. Resentment can also stem from selfish motives. Regardless of the reasons, offer your in-laws kindness and grace.

Then Embrace

Embracing in-laws when the relationship feels prickly is indeed challenging. Here are some practical steps and insights to navigate the dynamic:

1. **Show Genuine Interest**: Take time to learn about your in-laws' interests, hobbies, or values. Ask open-ended questions about their lives—maybe their favorite memories, hobbies, or even family traditions.

2. **Small Acts of Kindness**: Serve them in subtle, thoughtful ways. Offer to help with a task during a visit, like cooking or cleaning, or send a kind note or small gift.

3. **Set Healthy Boundaries**: Politely but firmly set limits if interactions feel toxic. For instance, if conversations get tense, redirect to neutral topics or excuse yourself calmly.

4. **Focus on Your Commitment to Your Partner**: Loving your partner includes embracing their family. View your efforts as an extension of your commitment to your partner, which can reframe the challenge as an act of love.

5. **Manage Expectations**: Temper your expectations. You can't control their response but you can control your mindset.

Even if they don't reciprocate, consistent kindness can soften your own heart. Over time, this may ease tension or at least help you feel at peace with your efforts.

To The Divorced Parent

I would be remiss if I didn't address divorce in relation to parenting. I have counseled hundreds of parents, and one of the most impressive duos I've worked with was a divorced couple. Here is their story. Their elementary-aged child struggled with behavioral issues, and the parents requested a session with me to support their child. I wasn't sure what to expect, as it's rare for divorced parents to attend a session together.

As I greeted them, I invited the parents to share their concerns. They explained that, although they had fallen out of love with each other, they were fully committed to minimizing the divorce's impact on their child. They supported each other as parents and never criticized one another. Both valued the other's role and remained united for their child's well-being.

The child's difficulties soon dissipated, making it one of the shortest cases I've handled. I didn't do anything magical; the magic lay in two parents who refused to use their child as a pawn. That alone was a tremendous gift to their child. I have no doubt that the child has adjusted well to life with two caring parents.

If you've been guilty of mistreating your ex, consider softening your stance. Your ex may have done terrible things to earn your anger, but unless you want your child to seek out toxic relationships, avoid modeling them. Children deserve both parents cheering them on through life.

My parents divorced when I was ten, and it was challenging for me. There was a time when I didn't want to visit my mother. I thought my dad would side with me, but he insisted I spend time with her. He respected her as my mother and encouraged me to do the same. I'll always admire how he treated her.

Struggles with Adult Children

Parents of adult children face unique joys and challenges. Unfortunately, some adult children make choices that sadden us. While most parents have regrets, you are not responsible for your adult children's choices. They have the agency to shape their lives, for better or worse. As they navigate struggles, you can offer love and guidance, but ultimately, they determine their own future.

Caregivers of Aging Parents

The cycle of life can bring us full circle with our parents. They once nurtured us when we were helpless, and we may have the opportunity to return the favor.

I've seen stable relationships implode under the stress of caring for aging parents. Recently, I met with a woman who was at her breaking point, overwhelmed and unable to function. She cried as she described being pulled in a thousand directions.

To help, I asked her to identify her primary concern at that moment. Her main source of stress was caring for an older family member, with transportation to his appointments being her biggest struggle. Together, we explored community services and found alternative transportation options for some of his appointments. We also developed a plan to delegate responsibilities to other family members. She left with a smile and a plan. Rejuvenated, she could prioritize self-care, which improved her ability to care for her loved ones.

If you're in this situation, safeguard your relationship with your partner by utilizing resources for your aging loved ones. Your personal efforts are remarkable, but no one should shoulder caregiving responsibilities alone.

Finding a Balance

Most of us are stretched thin by demands on our attention and time. Work, school, church, clubs, sports, parenting, or caring for extended family members can pull us in many directions. It's a lot to manage. Many of us, as people-pleasers, find it easy to say yes when asked to take on more tasks. But it's okay to say no.

"You can say no and you don't need to give an excuse."
—Jolene Crooks

Recognize when you're burnt out and share some of your burden. When you don't feel nurtured yourself, it's nearly impossible to give proper attention to your partner and others around you. Invest in your own self-care.

Take a Break

Sometimes, we become so entwined in parenting and caring for others that we struggle to remember what it was like to be a carefree couple. When you start viewing your partner more as a co-parent than a lover, it's time for a break.

When our children were young, we once left them with family members and checked into a hotel in our own hometown. It sounds silly, but we needed a break from parenting. With limited funds at the time, we couldn't afford a big vacation, but we thoroughly enjoyed playing as tourists in our hometown.

Taking breaks or vacations helps you refocus on your partner and allows your relationship to grow independently of your children. These breaks are also healthy for children, as they gain precious time with extended family or other loving caregivers.

Mantra

We will work together for the betterment of our family. We will find balance through unsettling times. As challenges with children or other family members arise we will encompass all with love and security.

Chapter 7
Appearance and Grooming

"Grooming is the secret to real elegance. The best clothes,
the most wonderful jewels; the most glamorous beauty
don't count without good grooming."

—*Christian Dior*

It's easy to neglect your appearance in a long-term relationship, but I encourage you to keep impressing your partner with your style throughout your journey together. Your appearance and fashion choices can boost your self-confidence. When I make an effort to improve my appearance, I also feel better about myself.

Like many, I found it easy to gain weight after settling into my relationship. Excess weight carries significant health risks, including obesity-related medical concerns. If you've noticed unhealthy weight gain, consider lifestyle changes. Most diets work if you stick to them, so the key is finding one you can sustain and enjoy for years.

Grooming 101

In the early days of dating, most of us were meticulous about our grooming—every hair in place, face freshly shaved, clothes stylish, and breath minty fresh! As time passes in a long-term relationship, it's easy to let these habits slip, but maintaining them can boost your confidence and keep the spark alive.

While not exhaustive, here's a list of key grooming areas to consider. Review it and give yourself a quick self-assessment:

- Body showered and clean
- Hair cleaned and cut as desired
- Facial and other hairs trimmed to preference
- Deodorant as appropriate
- Finger and toe nails trimmed
- Teeth brushed and flossed
- Breath freshened
- Clothing clean and tidy
- Makeup used appropriately
- Cologne or perfume applied conservatively
- Skin care products as appropriate

Fresh Style

Looking back at old photos, I can see times when my style was way off. It's easy to fall into a rut of wearing the same "comfy" clothes all the time. Be open to trying a new look, whether it's a fresh hairstyle, a revamped wardrobe, or any change to your appearance.

"You'd be surprised how much it costs to look this cheap!"
—Dolly Parton

Refresh your style by exploring new clothing options and spending time in the dressing room. You might discover new favorites that rejuvenate your wardrobe. If subtle changes in your style and appearance make your partner's heart flutter, why not give it a try?

Consider a date night where you shop together, trying on new clothes or jewelry. Be open-minded and experiment with items you wouldn't normally choose, like bold colors or unique styles. Embracing change, a key theme of this book, makes this the perfect opportunity to practice.

Be The Best You

People have different values about what constitutes appropriate grooming, and that's perfectly fine. While I have my own styles and standards, they may not align with yours. As I've encouraged you to try new clothes and looks, the key is to be the best version of yourself. Take pride in who you are!

Mantra

Caring for myself will allow me to take greater pride in my appearance. I don't need to compare my looks to anyone else, I am uniquely special and I will become the best me!

Chapter 8
Learning New Ways to Love by Embracing Change

"Me? I'm scared of everything. I'm scared of what I saw, I'm scared
of what I did, of who I am, and most of all I'm scared of walking
out of this room and never feeling the rest of my whole life the
way I feel when I'm with you."
—*Baby, Dirty Dancing*

Adjust, Adapt, and Overcome

Accepting change has been incredibly difficult for me. It can feel uncomfortable and even frightening to step into the unknown. Yet, change is the one constant in life, so we must learn to adjust, adapt, and overcome.

As a teenager, I attended just one concert at the local fairgrounds, where Jerry Reed performed. While I enjoyed hearing "East Bound and Down" (the *Smokey and the Bandit* theme), the huge crowds, ticket fees, and parking soured the experience. I decided buying music was better than dealing with those hassles.

A decade later, I went to another concert, dreading the parking, drive, and crowds. I enjoyed it no more than the first one. Looking back, I realize my negative attitude shaped my experience, I disliked it before even arriving.

Years later, I saw how much concerts meant to Jolene. I recognized my selfishness in avoiding them and had a change of heart. Jolene does so much to make me happy, so I committed to attending concerts with her, determined to enjoy them, even if it meant faking it at first. My goal was to make the experience special for her, no matter what.

At one concert, her radiant smile filled my heart. Seeing her so happy changed my perspective forever. Now, I take photos of her at concerts to capture the joy bursting from her face. Witnessing happiness in someone you love is a profound gift. In our often-selfish world, it's easy to forget to serve our partners without expecting something in return.

When you go all in to make your partner happy, you may unlock a more fulfilling relationship, a precious reward. While we shouldn't act solely for rewards, they sometimes come. The more excited I am about doing things Jolene enjoys, the more she embraces the activities I love.

Not All Change is Good but So Much Of It Is!

We should never force someone to change in ways they're not comfortable with. If you've been asked to change, reflect on whether your resistance stems from discomfort or a conflict with your values. If it's simply awkward for you, give it a try! A wondrous world awaits when you embrace new experiences.

"It is not the strongest of the species that survive, nor the most intelligent, but the one most responsive to change."

—*Charles Darwin*

In counseling, "successive approximations" refers to reinforcing behaviors that are close to the desired outcome. This means acknowledging your partner's baby steps as they try new things outside their comfort zone. Positive reinforcement is one of the most powerful motivators for change.

If you want your partner to hike with you but they're not ready for a mountainous climb, start with a short walk and build them up. You might say, "I know you don't feel ready to hike, but I'm so impressed with how you did today." Encouraging words foster confidence and facilitate lasting change.

A key takeaway from this book is this: Be willing to be uncomfortable! Feeling slightly uneasy means you're tackling something new or challenging. Most of us will extend grace when our partner steps out of their comfort zone. A while back, I realized Jolene's happiness meant more to me than my own comfort—a decision that transformed my life.

Prioritize your partner's happiness over your comfort. Jolene was nervous about trying dance lessons with me, yet she took a leap of faith, enduring my clumsy steps during the instruction. Her vulnerable yet determined expression as we danced made that day unforgettable. Our joy together stemmed from her willingness to embrace the uncomfortable.

Mind Over Misery

Recently, we spotted a theme park's towering roller coasters and reminisced about how, as children, those amusement park rides filled us with excitement. I recall being giddy at the thought of the fun awaiting inside. What if we approached activities with our partner with the same childlike enthusiasm? How can we do this? Through positive self-talk.

Self-talk shapes our mindset every day, often hundreds of times, yet most of us barely notice it. I don't recall my exact thoughts of pulling into a theme park as a child, but it was something like, "Wow, that new roller coaster will be a blast! I can't wait to feel the cold water of the log ride!" Can we channel that excitement into time with our partner? Yes! It starts with intentional self-talk.

Jolene once bought tickets to a *Clue*-themed murder mystery dinner. I wasn't thrilled about the idea, but I knew she was excited. Instead of just enduring it, I chose to embrace it. When Jolene suggested wearing *Clue*-inspired costumes and declared she'd be Miss Scarlet, I decided to be Colonel Mustard. As I planned my costume, I told myself, "This could be fun!" That simple shift in self-talk transformed the experience into a joyful, memorable evening.

This could be fun!

That subtle self-talk changed everything! We had a blast shopping for costume supplies and even planned a date night to rewatch the 1985 *Clue* movie for inspiration. By the time I strolled into the murder mystery dinner, I was confident we'd have a great time. Initially, I wasn't thrilled about Jolene's idea, so what changed? Positive self-talk shifted my attitude for the better. My Colonel Mustard costume even won best costume!

When we expect something to be terrible, it often is. But when we anticipate it being special and enjoyable, our positivity can make it pleasant, even if it's not perfect. Positive self-talk requires practice, especially on small things. Shifting your focus to what's good about a situation may be challenging, but it can infuse everyday life with joy and happiness.

The next time your partner invites you to try something new, tell yourself, "This could be fun!" Repeat it until you believe it. Those four words can transform your outlook and open you to adventure. Once you master that phrase, graduate to this one:

This *will* be fun!

There is no need to walk through life being miserable when things don't go your way. Find the positives. There are positives to almost every situation if you simply look. If you've looked and can't find positives, create them yourself!

Unconditional Service

Serving our partners unconditionally strengthens our relationships. When you offer kindness without expecting a reward, the relationship improves, even if your partner doesn't immediately reciprocate. Your selfless acts create a foundation for deeper connection.

Even if your partner doesn't seem to deserve your kindness in a particular moment, unconditional generosity fosters more kindness over time. Reciprocation may not happen instantly, it's like planting a seed. A seed doesn't produce fruit right away; it requires months of watering, weeding, and sunshine before yielding a harvest. Kindness begets kindness.

In most couples, one partner is often more motivated to grow and improve the relationship. Since you're reading this book, I assume you're that person. I empathize with your frustration if your partner isn't as eager to enhance your bond. Stay hopeful—your efforts matter.

With our plates overflowing, easing your partner's burden can make a big difference. For example, handling their car inspection or oil change can lift a tedious "to-do" item off their list. There are countless ways to serve each other, lightening the load and deepening your connection.

> "As we lose ourselves in the service to others we
> discover our own lives and our own happiness."
> —*Dieter F. Uchdorf*

The more you serve your partner, the more free time your partner will have. With chores out of the way, there is more time for connection. Here is a list of things you can try to give service to your partner. I challenge you to do every single one of these over the next year.

30 Ways to Give Service to Our Partner

1. Get the oil changed in their car
2. Bring them a cold drink without them asking
3. Turn down the bedding and sheets before bed
4. Prepare a surprise meal
5. Do the laundry and put it all away
6. Put away leftovers
7. Wash and vacuum their car
8. Give them a quick foot massage
9. Rush to help bring in groceries as they arrive
10. Surprise them with breakfast in bed
11. Listen intently when they share work or life stresses
12. Pack their lunch
13. Review their "to do" list and do something from it
14. Take on an unpleasant task (dishes or the bathroom)
15. Offer to make them a plate or drink at social events
16. Give them a full body massage
17. Walk the dog or care for other pets
18. Tidy the home
19. Wash the bedding and make the bed
20. Hear their expressed needs and work to address them
21. Help them unpack after a trip
22. Brush and play with their hair
23. Give them a "me day"
24. Fix that thing they've been nagging you to fix
25. Ask them if they need anything while you are shopping
26. Ask: "What can I take off your plate today?" and do it
27. Jump in and help with something they are working on
28. Give them a back scratch
29. Take care of all child related tasks for a day
30. Clean out and organize a closet or garage

Growing on a Date Night

All too often, couples fall into the same date night rut. After debating for an hour about where to eat, you finally decide and go. After the meal, you head back home. That's not a date night, that's just eating together in a public place. This isn't to say that an occasional dinner out is bad, but you should challenge yourselves to occasionally add a unique activity to your date nights. If you're hesitant to try something new, do it anyway! Plan a few days in advance to find fun activities. Social media is a great source of ideas for local events that can turn into date night gold. If you're struggling to come up with ideas, check out my list of 250+ unique dates. Don't overthink it—just pick a date and go for it!

The Special Date and the Ultimate Fantasy Dream Date

We often fail to realize what dates our partner wants, what dates mean the most. I made the following activity to help couples explain their deepest dating desires. There are two types of dates to consider: Special Dates and Ultimate Fantasy Dream Dates.

Special Dates

Special Dates are activities you dream of doing but haven't tried yet or unique experiences you haven't enjoyed in a while. For example, one of Jolene's Special Dates was ice skating, so I agreed to go. I was nervous, but the snow-draped Appalachian Ski Mountain set a magical scene. Sure, we fell a few times, but we laughed it off. By the end of our session, I enjoyed it even more than she did! Now it's your turn to pick your Special Dates—those experiences you usually only think about. Feel free to include small trips or special events. The key is that they're doable but outside your usual routine. Encourage each other to enthusiastically embrace your partner's Special Dates, and watch the magic unfold!

As you read over your partner's list, are you surprised at anything you see? Are the dates something you could feasibly do for them? Your partner's date ideas may be uncomfortable, but I encourage you to expand your comfort zone. If you do something your partner truly loves, you may enjoy it more than you can imagine. Even if you don't love the date, you are loving them which means everything!

The Ultimate Fantasy Dream Date

Now, let's dive deeper. What would you do if there were no limits—financial, logistical, or otherwise? Where would you go? What wild adventure or romantic experience would you share? This might be a once-in-a-lifetime dream, so let your imagination soar! Maybe it's a private dinner on a Parisian rooftop, a midnight safari in Africa, or a magical trip to ski the Swiss Alps. Share these dreams with your partner, and even if they stay dreams for now, you'll learn what makes their heart race.

Partner #1 _____

Elements of my Ultimate Dream Date…

-
-
-
-

Partner #2 _____

Elements of my Ultimate Dream Date…

-
-
-
-

Before writing this book, I asked Jolene to share her dream date, and I was stunned by her ambition. She envisioned a helicopter ride, a romantic dinner, and dancing to a live band. She didn't expect me to make it happen. After a year of planning, I whisked her away with first-class tickets to Nashville. We took a breathtaking helicopter tour, savored an exquisite dinner at Michael Mina's Bourbon Steak, and sat front row at Vince Gill and Amy Grant's concert. I hope she'll always cherish that as the greatest date of her life. It was her dream date, but I loved every second too! None of those activities were things I'd normally choose, yet they created some of my fondest memories.

Whatever your partner's dream dates are, why not try them? Your willingness to embrace their dreams shows your commitment, and your enthusiasm to make it fun and memorable reflects an even deeper love.

Mantra

As I expand my comfort zone I will become more flexible to new adventures. I will accept and embrace change. I will thrive!

Chapter 9
Growing Together and Time Apart

"Coming together is a beginning;
keeping together is progress;
working together is success."

—*Edward Everett Hale*

A strong relationship thrives on closeness and connection, and there are many ways to nurture this growth. Sharing hobbies and creating traditions are simple yet powerful ways to connect. Whether it's cooking together every Sunday or exploring a new hobby like dancing, these shared experiences build lasting memories and strengthen your relationship.

Hobbies are the activities we turn to for relaxation and joy, ranging from watching favorite television shows to thrilling adventures like skydiving. Some of my favorite pastimes include disc golf, comic books, and playing minigolf.

Hobby Time

To deepen your connection, try this fun activity: List your top four hobbies and guess your partner's top four favorite hobbies. Then, share and compare your answers. You'll spark meaningful conversations and discover new ways to enjoy time together!

Partner #1 _____

My hobbies:

1.

2.

3.

4.

My partner's hobbies:

1.

2.

3.

4.

Partner #2 _____

My hobbies:

1.

2.

3.

4.

My partner's hobbies:

1.

2.

3.

4.

Ready to grow closer through shared hobbies? Ask each other: Which hobbies would you like to try together? Be bold and join your partner in one of their favorite activities. It's okay if you're not as skilled, give yourself grace and avoid self-criticism if you struggle. These moments are about putting on a happy face and enjoying your partner's joy. Let them teach you about their passions. You might be surprised by how much you enjoy their company while doing something they love.

I enjoy disc golf, but when Jolene joined me, she struggled with her throws and grew frustrated. She hasn't returned to the course since, but I cherished her company as we roamed the park. Her frustration with her skills kept us from fully enjoying the day. Jolene may not know until she reads this, but I love when she watches me excel. Even after all these years, I want to impress her and make her proud. An adoring glance or flirty compliment from her lifts me like nothing else. She might feel inadequate playing sports, but by joining me, she sees me shine, which means the world to me. Though disc golf wasn't her thing, I admire Jolene's willingness to try.

When I invited Jolene to play pickleball, she hesitated after her disc golf experience but gave it a shot. Her tennis skills shone through, and now we've found a hobby we both love playing together! Trying each other's hobbies should be a two-way street as it wouldn't be fair if she tried mine but I ignored hers. Years ago, Jolene invited me to a craft night at a woodworking store. I was nervous, but I enjoyed making a wooden sign together. Every time I see that sign in our laundry room, I'm reminded of that fantastic date. I never imagined enjoying crafting, but because it mattered to her, it became important to me. I can't stress this enough:

If something is important to your partner, make it important to you!

When your partner invites you to share their hobbies, seize the opportunity. It's not just about participating, it's an invitation to their heart. A recurring theme in this book is stepping outside your comfort zone to boost your partner's happiness. When you prioritize their joy, you'll find your own happiness grows. Join each other's worlds, embrace each other's passions, and watch your connection deepen.

Traditions

Most of us cherish our unique traditions, which bring comfort and joy to our lives. My favorites include reading *Popcorn* by Frank Asch each Halloween, playing Stratego on Thanksgiving Day, and savoring "Yoda Soda" (lime sherbet mixed with lemon-lime soda) on New Year's Eve. These rituals fill my heart with happiness.

Sometimes, as hard as it may be, traditions must evolve or end. For years, our children slept together in one upstairs room on Christmas Eve, giggling and buzzing with excitement about the gifts awaiting them. Jolene and I relished our evening downstairs, arranging presents and nibbling on Santa's cookies. On Christmas morning, the kids waited at the top of the stairs for the green light, then stampeded down to the Christmas tree, marveling at the loot underneath. Those moments are priceless memories.

Those sweet young family Christmas days have passed. While our children may or may not carry on that tradition, we embrace the joy of those unforgettable years. Cherish your traditions, but hold space for new ones to grow.

Purposeful Change in Traditions

One Thanksgiving, Jolene surprised me with an impromptu trip to North Carolina's Outer Banks. I wasn't thrilled about breaking tradition, but I played along with an open mind. With the country celebrating at home, we had the lighthouses nearly to ourselves, enjoying a unique, chilly beach adventure.

No restaurants were open, and the only store was a small general store. I'll never forget our Thanksgiving lunch at the base of Cape Hatteras Lighthouse: chips, spray cheese, Beanie Weenies, and sodas. It was the worst Thanksgiving meal ever—and yet absolutely wonderful! That day taught me it's okay to step away from tradition and embrace new memories with your partner.

The New Normal

Change is life's one constant, and I'll admit, I often struggle to accept it. As couples journey through the years, adjustments are inevitable. Years ago, I learned about embracing "new normal," a concept that has helped me adapt to life's shifts. Essentially, it's about creating new norms and traditions when change comes. Health, income, housing, or relationships may shift, sparking new circumstances. Instead of clinging to the past, embrace these "new normals." Cherish old traditions fondly, but don't dwell on them—holding too tightly can lead to sadness. Welcome change as an opportunity to build fresh memories with your partner.

"Train yourself to let go of everything you fear to lose."
—*Yoda*

Why not embrace the positives in your current situation and get excited about creating new traditions? Flexibility can make new rituals a joy. My brother Tom, after living in Estonia, introduced us to a fun birthday tradition: the person being celebrated sits in a chair and gets playfully tossed up by family and friends. We've adopted this ritual, and it's now a highlight of every child's birthday. Welcome change and your "new normal" to create new, and joyful memories with your loved ones!

Alone Time

Escaping the daily grind to enjoy solo time can be incredibly refreshing. Jolene once took a trip to visit our daughter, relishing some much-needed downtime from family responsibilities, work, and even me! On her drive home, Jolene stopped for a meal and listened to her favorite podcast, returning home rejuvenated. When was the last time you carved out time for yourself? A little solitude can recharge you, strengthening your connection with your partner.

List some activities or moments that you prefer or enjoy doing alone.

Partner #1 _____	Partner #2 _____
1.	1.
2.	2.
3.	3.
4.	4.
5.	5.

Some hobbies are best enjoyed solo, and that's okay. I love attending collectible shows, happily wandering the aisles for hours. I prefer doing this alone, and Jolene doesn't need to join me. She appreciates my finds, but she has her own events she enjoys solo, and we welcome these differences. They keep us refreshed. Even in a loving relationship, we all need a break sometimes—and that's perfectly healthy. If distance makes the heart grow fonder, a little space can deepen your connection.

Growing Together Playing Board, Card, and Video Games

Games have been a cherished part of my life since I played Candy Land as a child. Over the years, I've enjoyed countless board, card, and video games, each adding joy to our family moments. Every year, we discover a few new favorites to add to our collection. I've compiled a list of our go-to games—the ones we always return to, for your consideration.

Board Games

Board games range from simple to delightfully complex. While some enjoy hours-long strategy sessions, most prefer games that wrap up in 30–90 minutes. My recommendations typically take an hour or less, perfect for family fun. Here's our family's go-to list of favorites that never fail to bring joy:

1. **Wingspan:** My all-time favorite. Collect birds in diverse habitats to earn points. Stunningly beautiful and endlessly replayable.

2. **Ticket to Ride**: An easy-to-learn railroad-building game. Race to complete routes before opponents, with excitement building every turn.

3. **Azul**: A fast-paced tile-laying game that's deeply satisfying. Hard to describe but consistently in our top three.

4. **Hey! That's My Fish!**: A cute, quick game where penguins collect fish while outmaneuvering opponents on a shrinking board.

5. **Carcassonne**: Jolene's favorite. Build castles and farm land by placing tiles, with each game feeling fresh and unique.

6. **King of Tokyo**: A fun mix of cooperation and competition. I love it, though my family needs convincing to play.

7. **Clue**: A quick deduction game. Our 1980s version shines, especially during Clue movie rewatch nights.

8. **Scrabble**: The classic word game that inspired digital hits like Words with Friends. Always a crowd-pleaser.

9. **Boggle and Super Big Boggle**: Shake letter blocks and race against the clock to form words in three minutes. A longtime family favorite.

10. **Tiny Towns**: A tense, quick game where you build homes and taverns to maximize points. Everyone stays engaged.

Card Games

Card games are portable, quick, and endlessly fun, often faster than board games. A simple deck of poker cards unlocks dozens of games, but our family also loves these card-based favorites for their unique charm:

1. **For Sale**: Buy and sell real estate, from lavish mansions to humble tents. Easy to learn and incredibly enjoyable.

2. **Jaipur**: A delightful two-player game with stunning artwork, where you collect gold, silver, rubies, and other goods.

3. **Flapjacks and Sasquatches**: A humorous, simple game filled with lumberjack antics as you chop trees and claim rewards.

4. **Munchkin**: A playful take on Dungeons & Dragons, perfect for unleashing your inner nerd. Not for everyone, but a blast for fans.

5. **Magic The Gathering**: A complex, ever-evolving game for dedicated gamers. Its depth and popularity are astounding, but it's not for beginners.

6. **Pokémon**: A charming game that's not just for kids. A simpler alternative to Magic: The Gathering, it's stood the test of time.

These card games bring laughter and connection, making them perfect for cozy nights or on-the-go fun with loved ones.

Group Games

Gather a few couples for a lively game night with these group games, perfect for sparking laughter and connection:

1. **Jackbox Games**: An extensive collection of digital games everyone loves. Played using your phone as the controller, they're incredibly easy to pick up and endlessly fun for groups.

2. **Sheriff of Nottingham**: A thrilling bluffing game that's simple to learn and a crowd favorite. Jolene always wins, hiding her cunning behind that innocent smile!

3. **Werewolf**: A fun deduction game where you hunt werewolves before they devour you. It's as entertaining to watch as it is to play.

Games are more than entertainment—they're a way to create lasting memories with loved ones.

Mantra

Life will be enjoyed more fully as I engage in hobbies and activities. While I can share these events with my partner, I will also enjoy time on my own. Traditions will be cherished yet flexible.

Chapter 10
In Sickness and Health

"Friendship, love, health, energy, enthusiasm, and joy are
the things that make life worth living and exploring."
—*Denise Austin*

Loving someone when life is easy comes naturally, but the truth is, every couple faces rough patches. Illnesses, uncontrollable circumstances, or heavy responsibilities can strain relationships, especially over time. These challenges test your bond, yet they also offer opportunities to grow closer. By facing hardships together with patience and support, you strengthen your love and build a deeper connection that endures life's storms.

Physical Illness

One Christmas, I was bedridden with illness, unable to join our family's traditions. Jolene carried on, upholding our Christmas rituals while checking on me to ensure I stayed hydrated. Despite her stress, her care made that difficult day a sweet memory. Her strength brought us closer, showing how love shines in tough times.

Illness can reveal a couple's deepest strengths. In hospitals, you'll see partners holding hands, offering tender comfort. Viewing your partner's lows as chances to serve them will strengthen your bond. Chronic illness may demand ongoing adaptation, sometimes permanently. With today's medical breakthroughs, there are often ways to improve your situation, even if full recovery isn't possible. See these challenges as opportunities to create a "new normal" together, deepening your connection.

Anxiety, Depression, Stress and Worry

Sensationalized media bombards us with devastating news and shocking images, often overshadowing the positive moments in our communities. When we consume toxic media, it's easy to fixate on events beyond our control, fueling anger, fear, or hate. Take a pause if this happens. I've spent too much time worrying about things I can't change, creating my own mental and emotional strain. My son, Grant, a wellspring of wisdom, shared this quote:

"A man who suffers before it is necessary, suffers more than is necessary."
—*Lucius Annaeus Seneca*

Recognizing what worry can't fix is a powerful way to reduce stress. I'm preaching to myself here—I know I'm not alone in piling on stress by fretting over things beyond my control. Ask yourself: Will worrying change this? If not, say it aloud and convince yourself to move on. Let's focus on what we can control, like improving ourselves and nurturing our relationships, and let go of the rest.

Another key to easing stress is filling your life with positivity. Surround yourself with uplifting people, joyful activities, and self-care practices. Who and what you embrace shape your well-being. We all have unique ways to manage stress, and over the years, I've learned diverse coping strategies. Here's a list of self-care tips to try. Experiment with a few to find what rejuvenates you and strengthens your connection with your partner.

26 Healthy Mind and Self Care Tips

1. **Shake It Out**: Stand up, shake your arms, and jiggle your body. It sounds silly, but you can literally shake off stress.

2. **Watch Funny Videos**: Laugh at bloopers or fails. America's Funniest Home Videos is my go-to, but watching my son Hunter whiff at golf balls at the driving range is a personal favorite.

3. **Sip Cool Water**: Take a few minutes to sip and savor cool water. This simple act can surprisingly calm your mind.

4. **Go Offline**: Turn off computers and devices. It might spike anxiety briefly, but it often leads to a calmer state of mind.

5. **Gratitude Journaling**: Jot down things you're thankful for in a quality notebook and reread past entries to lift your spirits.

6. **Affirmations**: Recite a daily affirmation or quote. My favorite is, "I can do hard things."

7. **News and Media Break**: Avoid news and social media for a few days. This can be one of the most calming strategies.

8. **Take a Walk or Hike**: Walk for physical and mental benefits. I've even paced circles in my house while listening to music or watching TV.

9. **House or Yard Work**: Get lost in cleaning or gardening. A busy body can distract an overactive mind while enhancing your home.

10. **Protect Your Sleep**: Set a consistent bedtime and avoid electronics in bed to improve rest and reduce stress.

11. **Give or Accept a Hug**: Hold a 10–20-second hug with someone for a comforting physical connection.

12. **Concentrated Breathing**: Take semi-deep breaths, hold, and release slowly for several minutes to calm your mind and body.

13. **Movie Time**: Escape into a fun movie or TV show. Jared Hess films, like Napoleon Dynamite, are highly recommended!

14. **Be Positive**: Avoid negative talk or gossip. Focus on kind thoughts and words about yourself and others.

15. **Let Go of the Past**: You can't change yesterday—focus on today.

16. **Purge**: Declutter clothes or items for a freeing feeling and a tidier living space.

17. **Stretch**: Try gentle stretches or sprawl on the floor to loosen up and release tension.

18. **Decaffeinate**: Take a break from caffeine to slow down anxiety. Consider giving it up for lasting calm.

19. **Draw or Color**: Channel energy into drawing or a coloring book, enjoying the nostalgic scent of crayons.

20. **Shower or Bubble Bath**: Relax with a warm or cool shower, or soak in a long bubble bath.

21. **Enjoy Sex**: This intimate connection with your partner reduces stress and meets emotional needs.

22. **Sit Outside**: Relax on a porch or in a park, soaking in the sights, sounds, and fresh air.

23. **Go Limp**: Lie on a bed or sofa, relaxing tense muscles. I carry stress in my face, and letting it relax eases tension.

24. **Just Say No**: Decline overwhelming responsibilities without guilt—it's okay to set boundaries.

25. **Read a Book or Magazine**: Choose a physical book or magazine to give your eyes a screen break.

26. **Play a Game**: Enjoy a video, board, or card game.

These self-care practices not only reduce stress but also recharge you, helping you bring your best self to your relationship.

Stress and worry are natural parts of life, sometimes even productive. The key is to manage them wisely, limiting their hold when they're not useful. Prioritize self-care to nurture your well-being, which in turn equips you to support your partner more fully. For a deeper exploration of managing emotional duress, check out my book, *The Anxiety Atlas and Depression Guide*.

Anxiety and Depression

Anxiety or depression may challenge one or both of you at some point, testing your resilience and bond. Here is guidance to support a struggling loved one:

1. **Use Optimistic Communication**: Say, "We'll get through this together," to foster hope and unity.
2. **Give Space When Needed**: Anxiety or depression may cause agitation. Offer space respectfully.
3. **Prioritize Self-Care**: Enjoy your hobbies or time with friends to stay balanced.
4. **Encourage, Don't Demand**: Invite your partner to activities like a game night, but respect their pace.
5. **Assist with Care**: Help monitor appointments and medications to support their treatment.
6. **Ask About Suicidal Thoughts**: Don't shy away from gently asking about suicidal thoughts or plans to ensure safety.
7. **Be Patient with Treatment**: The first treatment may not fit. Support your partner through trial and error.
8. **Navigate Setbacks Together**: Celebrate good days and offer unwavering support during tough ones.

Mental Illness

Mental illness can profoundly affect relationships and quality of life, sometimes straining family bonds. If you or your partner struggle with mental health, early and consistent intervention is crucial. Seek help promptly. While this book doesn't cover mental health treatments, I urge you to explore reputable resources. Many suffer silently for years, but today's advancing treatments offer hope. Start with your primary care physician for guidance or referrals.

Supporting each other through mental illness or emotional distress can be challenging yet deeply bonding. When I've faced struggles, Jolene's simple words, "I'm here for you. Things will be okay," bring profound comfort. Your presence and support can strengthen your relationship, creating a safe haven for healing together.

Addictions

Substance abuse comes in many forms and addiction can mar and poison relationships. When the addicted partner is sober, they can seem like their wonderful "old self " which can give false hope to loved ones. Almost rhythmically, relapses occur with more heartbreaking, sometimes fatal results.
The cycle of deception that accompanies substance abuse can leave permanent emotional scars. I know this all too well with personal and professional acquaintances. Often, there are underlying medical and mental health conditions that need to be uncovered and treated. Notify your doctor and other health care providers when battling addiction.

I once worked with a man who was controlled by alcoholism. He was poised to lose his house, his job, his wife, and his children. Thankfully, he found help and was fortunate to keep everything he loved. Once he broke the bonds of addiction, his wife proudly cherished him. His children looked at their father with admiration once again. Addictions can be overcome.

It is beyond the scope of this book to address you or your partner struggles with addiction. Please seek professional help.

"We're not alone if we are together."
—*Alan Crooks*

Healthy Lifestyles

Setting healthy goals together can strengthen your bond with your partner while enhancing your well-being. A nutritious diet not only promotes longevity but also adds vibrant years to your life. As we age, our bodies are less resilient to junk food, but a balanced diet supports vitality. My nutritionist, my father, and extensive research highlight foods that boost physical and emotional health. Try incorporating these into your meals to feel the remarkable impact on your body and mind:

1. **Leafy Greens (Spinach, Kale)**: Packed with vitamins and antioxidants, they support heart health and mood stability.

2. **Berries (Blueberries, Strawberries)**: Rich in antioxidants, they enhance brain function and emotional well-being.

3. **Nuts and Seeds (Almonds, Chia Seeds)**: Provide healthy fats and protein to sustain energy and reduce stress.

4. **Fatty Fish (Salmon, Mackerel)**: Omega-3s promote heart health and may decrease depression symptoms.

5. **Pickled Foods (Sauerkraut, Kimchi, Pickles)**: Promotes gut health.

6. **Avocados**: Healthy fats boost mood and keep you satiated.

7. **Legumes (Lentils, Chickpeas)**: High in fiber and protein, they stabilize blood sugar and improve mood.

8. **Greek Yogurt and Kefir**: Probiotics aid gut health, which is linked to emotional balance.

9. **Healthy Oils**: Avocado and Olive oil are ideal options for antioxidants and anti-inflammatory properties.

Vitamins and Supplements

Nutritional deficits can harm your physical health, often leading to emotional and mental health challenges. A balanced diet is key, but sometimes supplements are needed. Consult your doctor to identify vitamins or supplements tailored to your needs. Addressing these deficits not only boosts your vitality but also supports your emotional well-being, strengthening your ability to connect with your partner.

Exercise

Exercise doesn't have to mean gym sessions or fitness classes—it can be so much more. Walking together has become a cherished ritual for me, especially when high-intensity workouts aren't an option. Yard and housework also count, engaging a wide range of muscles while beautifying your home. These activities not only boost physical health but also foster emotional well-being.

Partner #1 _____

List four ways you prefer to get exercise:

1.   3.

2.   4.

Partner #2 _____

List four ways you prefer to get exercise:

1.   3.

2.   4.

It's perfectly fine to enjoy exercise independently, nurturing your own health. A strong body supports your well-being and enriches your shared life. As partners in life's journey, prioritize fitness, whether through solo walks or gym sessions, to make your time together vibrant and meaningful.

Keep Some Autonomy

While nurturing each other strengthens your bond, excessive care can diminish autonomy, which isn't always healthy. Support your partner with love, but remember: you are ultimately responsible for your own well-being. Balancing care and independence fosters a resilient relationship, allowing both of you to thrive.

"Love rests on two pillars: surrender and autonomy. Our need for togetherness exists alongside our need for separateness."

—Esther Perel

While well-intentioned support strengthens bonds, both partners should maintain autonomy by learning essential life skills. Over-dependence on a partner's care can leave you vulnerable after loss, struggling with tasks like paying bills, home repairs, or health management. Foster mutual care, but ensure you can thrive independently. This balance builds a resilient relationship, preparing you for life's challenges together or apart.

Through the Lulls and Dulls

Life is a unique journey for each of us, like a roller coaster with exhilarating highs and challenging lows. I call these lows "lulls and dulls"—those blah moments when we feel off. Most of us experience these multiple times, but thankfully, we often emerge from them naturally. By supporting each other through these moments, you and your partner can strengthen your bond, making the journey richer.

> **"There'll be ups and downs, smiles and frowns."**
> —*Snoop Dogg*

If your "lulls and dulls" persist unusually long or deepen into depression, consult your doctor to explore underlying causes. Most of us bounce back naturally, but if you don't, seek help promptly. When your partner faces these lows, offer patience, giving them extra space and grace. Express your care gently, strengthening your bond through understanding.

Should I Ever Give Up On My Relationship?

If you're reading this book, you hold hope for your relationship. Only you know when you've reached your limit and have nothing left to give. Every situation is unique. However, abuse is never acceptable. If you're in an abusive relationship, seek professional help immediately. Most communities offer support programs—reach out to them. No one should feel pressured to stay with someone who mistreats them.

If you recognize yourself as the abuser, it's not too late to change. Seek professional help to break abusive patterns. You may not erase past wrongs, but you can grow into a better person. Embrace the challenge: you can do hard things!

If your relationship is struggling, don't lose hope, try my tips and techniques to promote positive change. You have little to lose and much to gain. Improving a relationship takes time, dedicated effort, and persistence. This is your life, so weigh your options thoughtfully as you shape your future.

Mantra

Trials and tribulations will come but I will confidently continue my journey through life. When health or other concerns arise, so will I. I will endure all obstacles.

ROGER CROOKS

Chapter 11
Comparisons and Appreciation

"Do not let anyone steal your happiness.
Do not compare yourself to others."
—*Peter M. Johnson*

We all have flaws. Generally, we are hyper-aware of our own imperfections, but others rarely notice or care about them. We scrutinize ourselves more than anyone else does.

When I realized I wouldn't be 6' tall, I was disappointed because almost every male in my family is 6' or taller. One day, while at my grandfather's house, we walked down to his basement, and he hit his head on a low-hanging pipe. He had foam taped around it to protect himself. Thankfully, I missed the pipe, and I found a positive in being 5'9".

Why shouldn't I be content with my perceived flaws and embrace who I am? I could list many more of my perceived imperfections, but I've realized that almost everyone struggles with their own body image. Embrace the uniqueness that is you, including your flaws. Learn to love your imperfections.

> **"Things are beautiful if you love them."**
> *—Jean Anouilh*

While many celebrities conceal their perceived flaws, I love how some embrace them. Consider the facial mole. The list of celebrities with a mole is extensive and includes legends like Marilyn Monroe, Morgan Freeman, and Tina Louise. To these celebrities, their "flaws" set them apart from others. They make them special—they are beauty marks! We should see our own perceived flaws for their unique beauty too.

Fixable Flaws

There is a well-intentioned notion that you are perfect the way you are and shouldn't change for anyone. While I agree with the general idea, this view is narrow and flawed. The increasingly popular mindset of living life however you want and letting others deal with it can be toxic to you and your relationships.

Many flaws should be addressed and corrected. These can be physical, but personality flaws often have the most significant impact on relationship dynamics. Some of us need to change bad habits and erroneous thinking. I have adjusted some of my selfish tendencies to more fully enjoy my relationships. I believe that addressing these flaws leads to greater life satisfaction than expecting others to "just deal with it." Self-improvement is a wonderful thing.

Comparisons

We live in an age of constant comparison. It's easy to become discouraged by others' wealth, beauty, or popularity. Interestingly, we often compare ourselves to those who have more than we do, but rarely to those who are less fortunate. If we compared ourselves to those with less, we would realize how much we truly have.

> **"Being like everybody is the same as being nobody."**
> —*Rod Serling*

Envy is a destructive emotion fueled by bitterness toward those who have more than we do. There's a remarkably simple cure for this: genuinely celebrate others' successes. Why feel frustrated or angry when others thrive? Embracing radical happiness for others fosters joy in your relationships and peace in your life.

In third grade, I sat with friends during lunch, bonding over our G.I. Joe and Star Wars figures. Some were harder to find than others, but when I scored a rare one, there was no jealousy—only shared excitement. We cheered for each other! I miss those days when a small friend group felt genuine joy for one another's successes rather than envy.

Recently, an acquaintance invited me out on his speedboat. I could have coveted his boat, but as we sped across the lake, I smiled at his success. I may never own a boat like that, and that's okay. I sincerely appreciated him sharing the lake life with me.

Cheer for and embrace the success of others.
Cultivate radical happiness for those around you!

What do comparisons have to do with your partner? A lot. When one partner becomes overly jealous or resentful, it can erode a relationship. Such partners may lose appreciation for what they have, both as individuals and as a couple.

Gratitude

To combat comparison, cultivate appreciation for what you have in your life. We all have far more to be grateful for than we often realize. Record what you're grateful for in each category.

Partner #1 _____

People:
1.
2.

TV shows or movies:
1.
2.

Books:
1.
2.

Games (board, card, or video game):
1.
2.

Trips to these places:
1.
2.

Household Items:
1.
2.

Things about my home:
1.
2.

Hobbies or Talents:
1.
2.

Partner #2 _____

People:
1.
2.

TV shows or movies:
1.
2.

Books:
1.
2.

Games (board, card, or video game):
1.
2.

Trips to these places:
1.
2.

Household Items:
1.
2.

Things about my home:
1.
2.

Hobbies or Talents:
1.
2.

Your gratitude list should help you recognize the wonderful things in your life. Find joy in them. You are not inferior to anyone unless you allow yourself to feel that way.

You Are Envied Too!

There are aspects of you that others envy! If you struggle with low self-worth, this may be hard to believe. I've seen this play out many times. It's ironic how some of the things we don't appreciate about ourselves are envied by the very people we envy! Perhaps it's true that we always want what we don't have. Here are some examples.

House Size Comparisons

- **Small House Owner's Thoughts About Large House Owners:** *"They have such a huge, gorgeous house. I could throw a huge party there."*
- **Large House Owner's Thoughts About Small House Owners:** *"I bet their house payment is half of ours. That must be how they afford all those vacations."*

Body Type Comparisons

- **Full-Figured Person's Thoughts About Thin-Figured Person:** *"They're so skinny. I wish I could fit into clothes like that."*
- **Thin-Figured Person's Thoughts About Full-Figured Person:** *"I love their curves. They fill out those jeans in a way I never could."*

Do you see how we envy others when there's no need? Your relationships with your partner and everyone else you encounter can grow stronger when you avoid comparisons.

> "If you look at what you have in life, you'll always have more.
> If you look at what you don't have in life, you'll never have enough."
> —*Oprah Winfrey*

Embrace your strengths and love yourself for all the wonderfully unique things about you and your relationships! You are truly special!

Jealousy and The Fear of Missing Out

The fear of missing out (FOMO) is not new, but increased social media and screen time have amplified this hidden struggle to new heights. Some of us dislike missing out on the fun things others are doing. When this turns into jealousy, you're at the mercy of FOMO, risking negative feelings and unpleasant emotions. Here's what to look for:

- Spending increased time on social media
- Feeling jealous while viewing others' photos or posts
- Blaming your dissatisfaction on those around you
- Experiencing a noticeable drop in self-confidence and self-esteem

10 Tips to Overcome Jealousy and FOMO

1. **Count Your Blessings**: It's hard to be jealous of others' lives when you focus on the positives in yours.

2. **Be Happy for Others' Success**: Embrace "radical happiness" for others' good fortune.

3. **Avoid Comparisons**: Comparing homes, jobs, vacations, or even partners is a fast track to discontent.

4. **Volunteer and Assist Others**: Losing yourself in service fosters appreciation for the wonderful things in your life.

5. **Be Inclusive**: If you feel left out, create your own fun and invite others to join.

6. **Practice Positive Self-Talk**: What you think and say to yourself is powerful. Use a mantra to counter negativity, such as, "My life isn't perfect, but it's so good!"

7. **Seek Counseling or Medication**: If disappointment turns into depression, consider professional help.

8. **Say Yes**: Participating in activities can combat jealousy. Ironically, some people experiencing FOMO are the ones declining invitations. Say yes!

9. **See Beyond the Shine**: Recognize that social media is a highlight reel—everyone has struggles.
10. **Take a Social Media Break**: Unplugging from social media can be transformative.

With effort, you can overcome jealousy. Don't risk missing out on your wonderful life by dreaming about someone else's. Embrace today and find joy now!

Happiness is Today

We often look to the future for happiness, but it cannot be found there. Happiness exists only in the present moment and place. While it's natural to fantasize about the happiness a big raise, new car, or dream trip might bring, these things won't truly increase your joy. Life returns to normal, leaving you with the same level of joy or discontent as before. The long-awaited events we expect to bring happiness often fail to satisfy. So, where is happiness?

Happiness is in health, even if it's not perfect.
Happiness is in the good in others, even if they have faults.
Happiness is in the beauty of the earth, even on a rainy day
Happiness is in someone who loves you, even if it's only you.
Happiness isn't in possessions; it's in joyful contentment.
Happiness is recognizing how much you have, even if others have more.
Happiness can only be found today.

"You know we just don't recognise the most significant moments of our lives while they're happening. Back then I thought, well, there'll be other days. I didn't realize that that was the only day."
—Dr. Archibald 'Moonlight' Graham from Field of Dreams

Removing the bitterness of comparisons and cultivating appreciation for what we have can boost your overall satisfaction. Celebrate others' successes, take pride in what you have, and show appreciation to your partner consistently. Let go of comparisons and embrace life more fully!

Partner Responsibility Appreciation

Have you ever felt unappreciated for the roles and responsibilities of your relationship? Appreciation for your partner will grow as you switch roles from time to time. Complete the following:

Partner #1 _____

List several of your responsibilities:

List one responsibility your partner has that you wouldn't want to do:

List one responsibility you have that you want your partner to do for a week:

Partner #2 _____

List several of your responsibilities:

List one responsibility your partner has that you wouldn't want to do:

List one responsibility you have that you want your partner to do for a week:

Open yourself up to appreciating each other. Consider temporarily swapping one of your roles. You might enjoy a new responsibility and choose to take it on more often.

Rather than praising my hard work in the yard, Jolene has a habit of pointing out things I missed. This frustrated me, so I invited her to help in the yard. After a few hours of laboring together, she had no more criticisms. Either she realized how challenging the work was, or she did it so well there was nothing left to critique—perhaps both.

On the flip side, one year I agreed to prepare the entire Thanksgiving meal. When it was time to take the ham out of the oven, I accidentally bumped it into the vegetable casserole, and both spilled onto the oven door—a complete disaster. Now I appreciate Jolene's kitchen skills so much more.

Possessions I Really Love

One of my all-time favorite television shows is the classic 1960s *Gilligan's Island*. The castaways were stranded on an island, each bringing a few prized possessions. The Professor had his science books, Ginger had her Hollywood dresses, and Thurston Howell III had his beloved teddy bear and money.

Have you ever wondered which belongings or possessions mean the most to you? I designed "The Island" activity to better understand the possessions that matter most to you and your partner.

Imagine you're going to a deserted tropical island to live with your partner forever. Assume the weather is always perfect and that you have all basic necessities, including shelter, simple clothing, medical supplies, food, and water. List two personal items you would take for each category.

Partner #1 _____

Clothing: _____ & _____

Books: _____ & _____

Games: _____ & _____

Snacks: _____ & _____

Personal items: _____ & _____

Partner #2 _____

Clothing: _____ & _____

Books: _____ & _____

Games: _____ & _____

Snacks: _____ & _____

Personal items: _____ & _____

Are you surprised by any of the items your partner chose to take? Did you realize how much those possessions mean to them?

Have To or Get To?

How many times a day do you say you "have to" do something? When I paid attention, I realized how often I did. I also noticed others around me using the same phrase. Saying you "have to" do something implies it's an obligation, something you'd rather avoid. This is one of the most life changing things I am sharing in this book...always say "get to!"

It's remarkable how changing one word can shift your perspective. Consider these examples:

- I *have* to go to work. → I *get* to go to work.
- I *have* to go grocery shopping. → I *get* to go grocery shopping.
- I *have* to take Jolene out tonight. → I *get* to take Jolene out tonight.
- I *have* to mow the lawn. → I *get* to mow the lawn.
- I *have* to cook dinner. → I *get* to cook dinner.

It's a radical shift to focus on what you get to do. Those who can no longer do the things they once "had to" do often realize these seemingly tedious tasks were not tedious at all.

I've made it a rule to avoid saying "have to" in my life, and I challenge you to do the same. Always say "get to." Watch your life transform into one of peace, calm, and gratitude as you embrace all the things you get to do.

Mantra

In a world of comparisons I will confidently and proudly be myself. My self worth will not be measured by others' success or failure. I am incredibly special and unique.

Chapter 12
Something to Laugh About

"Laughter is an instant vacation."
—*Milton Berle*

Humor is one of the most attractive traits and helps many couples navigate challenging times. Laughing at ourselves and the situations we find ourselves in can be a significant benefit.

Years ago, we took our children hiking in Pisgah National Forest. On our trek down the mountain, a torrential rain poured from ominous dark clouds, soaking us completely. Back at the van, I stripped off most of my clothes to dry them. As we prepared to leave, Jolene and I decided to swap seats. I stepped out and ran around to the other side, only to find the van doors locked! Jolene, inside the van, was laughing hysterically.

There I stood, half-naked, as cars whizzed by on the highway. It was utterly embarrassing. The kids joined in, pointing and laughing at my desperate pleas to be let back in. After savoring her prank, Jolene finally unlocked the doors. The whole family roared with laughter, and I couldn't help but join in, chuckling at my awkward dash around the van.

What are a few funny stories that you share as a couple?

1.

2.

Growing a Sense of Humor

I have an acquaintance who never understands my humor. Sometimes he doesn't know that I'm teasing. Maybe I'm not as funny as I think I am or maybe he has a limited sense of humor, perhaps both.

Explain to your partner the things that make you laugh. Jolene loves funny pictures. Once I learned what made her laugh, I could send goofy photos to her. I've grown my humor to match hers.

While on a trip to Oklahoma, Jolene gagged in the bathroom while brushing her teeth. She may have yelled obscenities too! I buckled over in laughter as she showed me what happened. She accidentally used antifungal ointment instead of toothpaste! All day she complained about the taste in her mouth and I laughed every time! Even now we joke about it. I love that she can laugh at herself.

I caution the more jovial partner to be sensitive to particular situations. There are times that positivity and humor just isn't appropriate. I'm guilty of trying to add humor to situations where it doesn't need to be. Use common sense as you determine when is and isn't an appropriate time for humor.

Lovely Laughter

Numerous studies highlight the value of laughter, but I've personally felt the joyful release of tension when I laugh heartily at something I enjoy. Shows like *King of Queens*, *Hogan's Heroes*, and *Sanford and Son* never fail to coax laughs out of me. My friend Steve is one of the few people who can effortlessly make me double over with uncontrollable laughter.

> **"A day without laughter is a day wasted."**
> —*Charlie Chaplin*

Lemons to Lemonade

Humor is a fantastic way to turn life's lemons into lemonade, but reframing challenges into positives is also a powerful tool in relationships.

John Edwards, a renowned therapist in North Carolina, was celebrated for his work with families. He had a remarkable gift for finding the positive in every situation. I was incredibly fortunate to train under him.

In one of my favorite demonstrations, Edwards sat surrounded by us participants and asked us to share challenging situations or statements we'd heard from the families we worked with. He would then transform the negative into a positive—it was remarkable. Here are a few examples:

Participant: "I stay up half the night worrying about him."
Edwards: "You are deeply invested in his well-being."

Participant: "She does whatever the hell she wants."

Edwards: "She is fiercely independent and determined."

Participant: "I don't know how much more I can take."

Edwards: "You have shown incredible patience."

Edwards continued this activity until we realized we could help our families (and ourselves) soften the negative and highlight the positive. In the counseling world, this is called a strengths-based approach. His demonstration left a lasting impact on me. Over the years, I've been complimented by others for using this simple technique. Always look for the positive intentions behind your partner's actions, as they're often hidden beneath puzzling behavior or cryptic words.

Daily Smiles and Laughter

Life can sometimes weigh us down, making it hard to find things to laugh about. I encourage you to smile every day. Try it right now: flash a big, wide smile. Fake it if you need to. Now, laugh—hard enough to shake your belly a bit. Fake it if you must. When I do this, I feel a surge of positivity, and I hope you do too. Seek out opportunities to smile and laugh throughout your day, and you'll reap positive mental health benefits. Look for sweet and funny moments—they're hiding everywhere!

Mantra

Laughter and humor lighten my day and gladden my heart. I have the ability to laugh at myself and enjoy the laughter and humor of others.

Chapter 13
The Financial Dance

"You must gain control over your money or
the lack of it will forever control you."

—*Dave Ramsey*

When Jolene and I were dating, we were swept up in that puppy love most couples experience. One of us even said we'd be happy living together in a tent in the woods. While it was a sweet sentiment, it was true only in the heat of the moment.

Maslow's Hierarchy of Needs captures it perfectly: basic needs like shelter and food must be met before higher needs, such as relationships, love, and belonging, can flourish. Love alone isn't enough. A solid financial foundation is crucial, as money management is a common source of stress in many relationships.

Spend Less Than You Make

Successful money management boils down to one simple phrase: spend less than you earn. It's truly that straightforward. By spending less than you make, you'll have funds for savings, investments, and emergencies. When financial challenges arise, you have two main options: earn more or spend less. Both are effective ways to improve your financial health, and combining them can yield faster results.

Education and Training

Pursuing education is typically a worthwhile investment. This includes formal education at a college or university, as well as trade schools and apprenticeships. Community colleges are an excellent starting point for both paths, with tuition costs often a fraction of those at larger institutions. Whether you choose traditional education or a trade, both can lead to greater financial freedom and stability.

Separate Accounts?

Because we both have incomes, Jolene and I divide financial responsibilities in a way that is fair to both of us, and we maintain separate bank accounts. For this to work, each partner must be mature enough to manage their money responsibly and cover their assigned bills.

The odd purchases we make don't bother the other person since we're not seeing deductions from our own accounts. Separate accounts have also made it easier to surprise each other with gifts or trips.

While separate accounts aren't popular among most relationship "experts," who often recommend joint accounts, they work for us. Joint accounts may be best for many couples, but they might not suit you. Do what's best for your relationship.

Emergency Savings Account

The best financial advice we received as a young couple was to establish an emergency account. This is a small pool of money set aside for unexpected expenses. We call ours a "freedom account" because it gives us peace of mind. Many couples feel they can't spare any money for an emergency fund, but they can! If you can afford to eat at a restaurant even once, you have enough to start. Begin small, but begin! Just $10 or $20 per pay period adds up faster than you think.

"Do not save what is left after spending, but spend what is left after saving."
—*Warren Buffett*

An emergency fund safeguards your financial well-being and prepares you for life's unexpected challenges. Set a goal to save $500 in your emergency fund. Once you reach that milestone, keep going. Saving $1,000–$2,000 can cover home repairs, appliance replacements, or car troubles. Building it to $5,000 or more brings an incredible sense of financial security. If you dip into your emergency fund, start replenishing it immediately.

28 Money Saving and Financial Tips

Over the years, I've learned numerous tips to save money, manage finances, and stretch our resources. Hopefully, these tips will work for you too!

1. **Pack Your Lunch**: Packing your lunch and skipping some restaurant meals can boost your bank account immediately. You might eat healthier too! It takes a bit of planning, but the savings are impressive.

2. **Sleep on Big Purchases**: Take time to weigh the pros and cons of major purchases. Avoid rushing into expensive decisions.

3. **Avoid Loaning Money**: Few things strain relationships faster than lending money. If you must help, consider giving it as an unconditional gift, but encouraging self-reliance is often best.

4. **Spending Freeze**: During a spending freeze, skip shopping or dining out and live off what you have. You'll be back in a surplus before you know it.

5. **Grocery Shopping Shutdown**: Occasionally pause food purchases (restaurants and groceries) for a few weeks. This saves money and helps rotate pantry items.

6. **Haircuts and Personal Care at Home**: Early in our marriage, Jolene and I brainstormed ways to stretch our dollars, and she started cutting my hair. We bought a $20 haircut kit, and on her first try, she gasped, "Oh my gosh, I'm so sorry!" after leaving a bald spot—she still laughs about it. I nervously let her hone her skills. Home manicures and pedicures also save money when funds are tight.

7. **Love on a Limited Budget**: Find cheap or free entertainment like visiting state parks, hiking, playing tennis, attending community events, watching movies at home, or playing games.

8. **Free Childcare**: Swap babysitting with other families for a free break. Grandparents are often eager volunteers.

9. **Try a Lunch Date**: Our favorite restaurant's lunch specials are nearly half the price of dinner. When possible, opt for a lunch date.

10. **Adjust Your Heat and Air**: Set the air conditioning a few degrees higher and the heat a few degrees lower. Ceiling fans can keep you comfortable.

11. **Stock Up During Sales**: Buy sale items your family already uses, choosing those with the longest "best by" dates. Stock up on food, toiletries, cleaning supplies, or personal hygiene products.

12. **Couponing**: Use coupons only for products you need or use. Many are available online or through apps.

13. **Avoid Buying New Cars**: Prioritize dependability and low mileage when buying cars. These are among your biggest purchases, so choose wisely.

14. **Cut the Cord**: Explore free or low-cost streaming services. Near big cities, an antenna offers free access to major networks and quirky channels.

15. **Thrift Stores**: When money's tight, thrift stores offer great clothes and treasures. Thrifting is now trendy too!

16. **Vegetable Gardening**: For self-sufficiency enthusiasts, gardening is a fun hobby. Start small! Check out *The Encyclopedia of Country Living* by Carla Emery for guidance.

17. **Buy Things During the Off-Season**: Purchase seasonal clothes or items when stores clear out old stock for the new season.

18. **Sell Unwanted Items**: Clear out clutter and earn cash online or at garage sales. Donate unsold items. Sell furniture, clothes, or collectibles online—you'd be surprised how much cash is hiding in plain sight.

19. **Choose Matinee Movies**: Early movie showings are cheaper. For bigger savings, wait for second-run theaters, streaming services, or the library.

20. **Loyalty Programs and Incentives**: Earn free nights or perks with loyalty programs. Scanning a loyalty card or app can yield significant discounts.

21. **Purchase High-Quality Items**: Cheap items often need replacing, negating savings. I use *Consumer Reports* to ensure I'm buying quality.

22. **Pay Off Debt**: Paying off debts saves on interest and fees, paving the way for true financial independence. Be cautious about taking on new debt.

23. **Buy in Bulk**: Purchase non-perishable goods you'll definitely use in bulk, but be selective to avoid waste.

24. **Museum, Zoo, or Aquarium Memberships**: A membership offers unlimited access to local museums, zoos, or aquariums, often with reciprocal benefits at other locations.

25. **Season Passes**: Season passes provide unlimited entry to amusement parks, water parks, or attractions, often with perks like free parking.

26. **Keep All Receipts**: I store receipts in an annual envelope. This helps with returns or disputes, like restaurant overcharges. During tax season, I sort and discard most.

27. **Follow Your Favorites**: Follow restaurants and venues on social media or sign up for email notifications to catch deals and save money.

28. The Magic Touch: Look at items you've bought and ask: "If I could touch this and get my money back, would I keep it or sell it?" Apply this "Magic Touch" test to future purchases.

Retirement Savings

Invest early and often in retirement savings. Couples who invest in their future gain far greater financial flexibility to enjoy life later on. Financial expert Kurt Reid promotes the simple "EARN + SAVE + INVEST + REPEAT" model which I heartily endorse.

Even if you can only contribute a small amount, start now. Early investments grow exponentially over time. I prefer the Roth 401(k) and Roth IRA as my primary retirement tools, but you should weigh the pros and cons for your own situation. Whatever you choose, begin saving today.

> **"Wealth accumulation seldom happens by accident. It happens by being disciplined and consistent while taking specific and intentional actions."**
>
> —*Kurt Reid*

Your investments may dip in value as the stock market reacts to economic and political factors. Financial professionals I consult recommend riding out market declines. Some even suggest investing more during downturns, as you can buy shares at a lower price. Resist the urge to withdraw from retirement accounts prematurely. Treat retirement savings as untouchable.

Life Insurance

Life offers no guarantees. Though it's uncomfortable to discuss, preparing for unexpected events like job loss, reduced income, disability, or even death is essential.

> **"If a child, a spouse, a life partner or a parent depends on you and your income, you need life insurance."**
>
> —*Suze Orman*

Research your family's insurance needs carefully. For life insurance, I prefer term life plans, despite insurance agents often promoting whole life policies.

Wills

Everyone should have a will that clearly outlines their final wishes. A will allows you to direct the distribution of your assets and ease your family's burden during a difficult time. It's unfair to leave loved ones grappling with uncertainty about your wishes while grieving.

It may seem unusual, but I make it a practice to share details of my will with my family to avoid surprises or hurt feelings. For example, my daughter Taylor asked to inherit my grandfather's hammer—done!

Finances: A Deeper Dive

For a deeper dive into personal finance, I highly recommend studying *The Total Money Makeover* by Dave Ramsey and *Financial Freedom Simplified* by Kurt Reid. If you're struggling to make ends meet, start with Ramsey's approach to build a solid foundation. Once you've mastered the basics, explore Reid's book for advanced strategies. Both books have significantly enhanced my life, providing a greater sense of financial security.

Important Document Placement

Keep important documents in a designated spot. These include birth certificates, Social Security cards, vehicle titles, and similar items. Consider using a heavy duty fire proof case or perhaps a brightly colored folder that is easy to locate.

Mantra

I can govern my spending while investing in my future. I am optimistic about my economic security and the achievement of financial freedom.

Chapter 14
Sexual Connections

"When I'm good, I'm very good,
but when I'm bad, I'm better."

—*Mae West*

Sex and intimacy mean different things to different people, so it's no surprise that this can become a source of heated contention and frustration. Too often, sexual needs go unmet because we struggle to communicate these desires effectively to our partners. While we might wish our partners could read our minds, they can't. We must provide them with a clear map and be patient as they navigate it.

Sexual Fulfillment Gauge

This tool encourages open communication between partners to enhance mutual understanding and fulfillment in your intimate relationship.

Partner #1 _____

Past Week Reflection: What have you done in the last week to support your partner's sexual fulfillment?

Looking Ahead: What could you do next week to further enhance your partner's sexual fulfillment?

Partner #2 _____

Past Week Reflection: What have you done in the last week to support your partner's sexual fulfillment?

Looking Ahead: What could you do next week to further enhance your partner's sexual fulfillment?

Low Desire, How to Turn Up the Heat

In addition to understanding our partner's sexual needs, it's equally important to match their enthusiasm for intimacy. It can be painful to desire a passionate sexual connection only to receive a lukewarm response. Those with lower desire can find ways to show their partner they're attuned to intimate, loving moments.

Intimacy Investment: Tips to Become More Involved

Strengthening intimacy in your relationship requires intentional effort and presence. These tips can help you deepen your connection with your partner, fostering a stronger bond through shared moments of closeness.

1. **Value Your Partner's Importance**: Acknowledge how much your partner means to you. Reflect on their role in your life and express appreciation, which lays the foundation for deeper intimacy.

2. **Understand the Importance of Intimacy to Your Partner**: Recognize that intimate time may hold unique significance for your partner. Listen to their needs and desires to ensure you're aligned, as open communication is key.

3. **Set the Mood and Be Present**: Create an atmosphere conducive to intimacy, whether through a quiet evening, soft lighting, or meaningful conversation. Stay fully engaged, free from distractions, to show your commitment.

4. **Create Special Moments of Intimate Bonding**: Plan intentional moments to connect, such as a cozy date night at home, a heartfelt talk, or small gestures that show love and care. These moments build lasting closeness.

The Power of Feeling Desired in Relationships

Few of us have felt desired all the time. At 14, I was awkward and struggled with dating, facing rejection that deeply wounded my self-worth. This period was filled with frustration and despair.

Thankfully, I blossomed by 17. Working at a classy restaurant, I was flattered when young women asked for my phone number or wanted photos with me—a stark contrast to earlier years!

Reflecting on these experiences, I see how being desired (or not) led my mind down two distinct paths. There's a domino effect that impacts us emotionally, for better or worse, based on the desire we feel from our partners:

- Sexually Neglected → Self-Doubt → Depression
- Sexually Pursued → Self-Confidence → Happiness

While on a trip without Jolene, I sent her a selfie of myself dressed up. She texted back enthusiastically, insisting she would frame that photo for her desk. My heart soared! Her small gesture boosted my confidence and made me feel deeply desired.

Consider how pursued or neglected your partner may feel. They might need a boost only you can provide. Pursuing your partner sexually—through hugs, passionate kisses, verbal expressions of desire, or showing they're your everything—infuses them with an indescribable confidence.

Enhancing Intimacy Through Open Communication

Improving intimacy in the bedroom starts with tactful communication of your preferences. Choose your words carefully, as many people feel sensitive when their intimate abilities seem critiqued.

If your partner has been open about their intimate desires, consider yourself fortunate. Their honesty isn't a criticism, it's a treasure map to their deepest wishes!

Praise your partner when they touch or engage you in ways you enjoy. Be specific about what they're doing well, as positive reinforcement is powerful. Open communication can ease many relational frustrations.

While physical attraction can be exciting, it may not be deeply fulfilling on its own. The greatest reward of a long-term committed relationship is gazing into the eyes of someone you adore and love on all levels, beyond fleeting moments of sexual attraction.

Prevent an Affair by Having an Affair with Your Partner

Physical and emotional affairs can devastate relationships. Is it possible to protect your partnership from the pain of an affair? Common elements of an affair include engaging conversation, intense interest, flirty texts, playful photos, impromptu dates, and exciting intimate encounters.

I challenge couples to actively "have an affair" with each other! The passion of early dating doesn't have to fade. As responsibilities like work, family, and other demands grow, don't let them dim the excitement of your romantic relationship.

Try these "affair" strategies to reignite passion with your partner:

1. **Participate in Engaging Conversation**: Share stories, dreams, or funny moments to deepen your connection.

2. **Show Intense Interest**: Ask about their day, passions, or desires, showing they're your priority.

3. **Send Flirty Texts**: Drop a playful or romantic message to keep the spark alive.

4. **Share Playful Photos**: Send a fun selfie or a suggestive snap, like a wink or a suggestive smile.

5. **Plan Impromptu Dates**: Surprise them with a snack run or a walk in the park.

6. **Create Exciting Intimate Encounters**: Set the mood with candles, music, or a special moment to rekindle intimacy.

There are no foolproof ways to prevent an affair, but making your partner your "personal affair" can help shield your relationship from outside threats.

Recently, I planted a Carolina Reaper pepper plant next to a Habanero. I gave the Reaper extra care, more compost, fertilizer, and attentive watering and weeding. By season's end, the Reaper towered over the Habanero with triple the peppers. This taught me a clear lesson:

The grass is greener where it's nurtured.

The relationship you prioritize and nurture will flourish. Make your partner your focus, give them your special attention.

The Love Languages of Sex?

Many couples try to meet their partner's sexual needs by offering what they themselves enjoy or assume their partner wants. When was the last time you provided your partner with a tailored, intimate sexual experience? If you can't recall, ask them. Don't take offense but be grateful for their insight, as it's a roadmap to their desires.

When exploring preferred intimate and sexual encounters, you or your partner may encounter acts that feel uncomfortable. While I encourage each partner to step slightly outside their comfort zone to enhance connection, no one should feel pressured to do anything they're morally opposed to. My hope is that both partners can feel satisfied and fully enjoy a personalized, fulfilling sexual relationship.

The Sexual Dream Date

Building on the Special Date activity, this exercise invites you to explore your intimate desires with your partner. By sharing your dream intimate or sexual experience, you provide a roadmap to deepen your connection and enhance your relationship.

Partner #1 _____

What would your dream intimate or sexual experience be? Describe this experience in detail.

Partner #2 _____

What would your dream intimate or sexual experience be? Describe this experience in detail.

With your partner's response in hand, you hold a powerful tool to strengthen your relationship. Use this insight to create meaningful, personalized moments that foster closeness and fulfillment.

Building Intimacy Through Respect and Connection

The quality of an intimate relationship is shaped outside the bedroom. How partners treat each other in everyday life significantly affects their responses to sexual advances and the overall depth of intimate experiences.

I once counseled someone who felt verbally berated by their partner during the day, yet at night, the same partner sought intimacy. Unsurprisingly, the connection was absent—and rightfully so. A healthy sexual relationship cannot thrive without first establishing mutual respect and shared understanding.

"In a great romance, each person basically
plays a role that the other really likes."
—*Elizabeth Ashley*

Daily life's demands can lead to differing energy levels between partners. Work and family responsibilities can leave us overwhelmed, draining the energy needed for intimacy. On such exhausting days, set aside your own desires and offer your partner unconditional love and support. These acts of care strengthen your bond and nurture your relationship.

Protect Time for Intimacy

Carving out intimate time at home can be challenging with children in the household. Consider designating a specific evening when children are away, giving you and your partner uninterrupted time together. They could spend this time visiting friends, staying with extended family, or engaging in activities outside the home.

Encourage children and teens to respect boundaries for your one-on-one time with your partner. Making your bedroom a private, intimate space, rather than a family gathering place, can deepen your connection. Prioritize and protect your intimacy to strengthen your relationship.

Mantra

I will cherish and honor my partner. Intimacy is a gift I'll care for and nurture as I grow my capacity to give and accept mutually gratifying sexual connection.

Chapter 15
Love Me the Way I Want to Be Loved

~

"Love is something you do for someone else,
not something you do for yourself."

—Gary Chapman

Love is a word with countless meanings. When I tell Jolene I love her, she interprets it through her own understanding of "love," which likely differs from mine. How do we discover what love means to our partner? Open communication is the key—ask, listen, and share to deepen your connection.

Chapman's Five Love Languages

Dr. Gary Chapman's The 5 Love Languages explores how couples express and receive love differently. Through years of counseling, Chapman identified five key love languages: Quality Time, Receiving Gifts, Acts of Service, Physical Touch, and Words of Affirmation. For a deeper understanding, I recommend reading his book, *The 5 Love Languages.*

At relationship seminars, I often share Chapman's framework and two personal anecdotes about how Jolene and I learned the hard way that loving each other in our way, not our partner's, can miss the mark.

Missteps in Love

Early in our marriage, I wrote Jolene a heartfelt poem, pouring my soul into it despite not being an elegant writer. I eagerly watched her read it, but days later, I found it in the trash. Heartbroken, I confronted her, asking, "Didn't you like the poem?" She replied, "It was great, I said thank you!" To her, it was a sweet gesture but not something to keep. I learned Jolene wasn't moved by poetry the way I was, revealing our differing love languages.

Conversely, I was the "villain" when the Nintendo Wii launched. Money was tight, and Wiis were scarce, so I had no hope of getting one. Jolene surprised me at work, beaming as she revealed a brand-new Wii. Instead of gratitude, I said, "Thanks, but we can't afford this," crushing her excitement. Looking back, I was a total jerk.

We both showed deep love but in our love languages, not each other's. These missteps taught us a vital lesson: we all have unique ways of feeling loved, and our partner's love language likely differs from ours.

Hitting the Sweet Spot

Years later, we got it right. At a furniture store, Jolene loved a large ottoman but hesitated due to cost and logistics. After she left for work, I secretly bought it, squeezed it into our van, and hid it in the attic until Christmas. When I surprised her, she was overjoyed—no poem could have melted her heart like that gift. As someone who isn't a natural gift-giver, I learned Jolene's love language—Receiving Gifts—and saw how thoughtful surprises light her up. It made me a better gift-giver.

For me, Jolene hit the mark with a tiny homemade book, 101 Reasons I Love Roger. She listed 101 things she loves about me, paired with photos from our life together. This sentimental gift filled me with love in a way the Wii never could, speaking directly to my love language—Words of Affirmation. Our success came from understanding each other's love languages: I crave romantic, sentimental gestures, while Jolene thrives on thoughtful surprises, experiences, and gifts.

Loving Intentionally

It's natural to give the love you want, but that approach often falls short. Retraining yourself to love your partner in their preferred ways can be challenging but gets easier with practice. Knowing what they want isn't enough, take purposeful actions to meet their needs.

Jolene and I still express love in our own languages. I leave her love notes and poetry, and she buys me tokens of affection or plans quality time. Now, we understand these gestures as expressions of deep love, even if they're not our preferred language. By focusing on your partner's love language, you not only meet their needs but also grow in your ability to love and be loved.

What you find romantic and heartfelt may differ from what your partner finds special. Discover their love language through open conversation or tools like Chapman's book and speak it intentionally. The rewards of this effort will deepen your connection and strengthen your relationship.

The Love and Enjoyment Survey

Understanding how to best love your partner starts with hopeful and heartfelt communication. To make this easier, I've created a simple survey to help partners share their preferences and desires, fostering a deeper connection through mutual understanding.

Partner #1 _____

- I would enjoy going: _____
- I would feel extra loved if: _____
- I would love to see you wearing: _____
- A way to excite me would be to: _____
- Somewhere we've not been to in a while is: _____

Partner #2 _____

- I would enjoy going: _____
- I would feel extra loved if: _____
- I would love to see you wearing: _____
- A way to excite me would be to: _____
- Somewhere we've not been to in a while is: _____

By completing and sharing this survey, you gain insight into your partner's unique ways of feeling loved, helping you tailor your actions to strengthen your relationship.

Celebrating Your Partner's Strengths

While learning to love each other in your unique ways, take time to appreciate the strengths you already bring to the relationship. List several things your partner does exceptionally well. These can include relationship strengths, work ethic, self-discipline, acts of service, personal care, or any other qualities you admire.

Partner #1 _____   **Partner #2** _____

My partner is really good at: My partner is really good at:

_____   _____

Positive Acknowledgement Love Tip

Everyone loves being recognized for their strengths. Take note of what your partner does well and share your appreciation. Creative ways to express your praise include verbal compliments, handwritten notes, social media shoutouts, or thoughtful texts. Celebrate their awesomeness!

Set a Reminder!

Understanding how your partner wants to be loved is only the first step. To deepen your relationship, you must act on that knowledge. With daily distractions and competing priorities, I've found that using a calendar helps me keep Jolene first.

Jolene once mentioned her dream of attending Vince Gill and Amy Grant's Christmas concert at the Ryman Auditorium. I joined Vince Gill's Fan Club for presale ticket access and set a calendar reminder. When tickets went on sale months later, that alert helped me secure two front-row seats. Using reminders builds habits to prioritize your partner's needs and desires. Don't rely on memory, set alerts now. Your partner is worth it!

Romancing 101

Romance comes naturally to some, but it's a challenge for others. Tension arises when a romantic and an unromantic partner come together. What does romance mean to you?

Partner #1 _____

Romance to me looks like:

I've shown romance to my partner by:

Partner #2 _____

Romance to me looks like:

I've shown romance to my partner by:

Being romantically mismatched can be frustrating, but understanding and acting on your partner's vision of romance can bridge the gap. For some, romance is poetry; for others, it's lingerie or holding hands on a beach. We each have unique romantic wishes and desires.

If romance matters to your partner, make it a priority. Share your romantic preferences with grace, not judgment or resistance. Meeting your partner's romantic needs boosts their life satisfaction and strengthens your bond. Your partner is worth the effort!

The 5 Steps to Increase Romance

Romance can be learned and nurtured through intentional effort. These five steps—communication, reminders, practice, follow-up, and enjoyment—can help you deepen your connection and make your partner feel truly valued.

1. **Communication**: Share what romance means to each of you. Create a list of romantic gestures that resonate personally. Open, honest dialogue sets the foundation for meaningful actions.

2. **Reminders**: Use tools like calendar alerts to prioritize romantic gestures. Reminders build habits to keep romance alive.

3. **Practice**: If romance doesn't come naturally, it may feel awkward at first. Keep practicing—whether it's writing a love note or planning a special date. Over time, these actions become easier and even enjoyable.

4. **Follow-Up**: If you're the partner craving more romance, acknowledge your partner's efforts with praise, even if they're not perfect. Positive reinforcement encourages growth and shows appreciation.

5. **Enjoy the Experience**: Embrace the joy of romancing your partner. You may discover that making them feel loved brings you fulfillment.

Wanted and Desired

Feeling valued is a core human need, and romance plays a key role in meeting it. To make your partner feel truly special, focus on these four essential areas:

- **Emotionally Comforted**: Show empathy and support to create a safe, loving space.
- **Physically Admired**: Express appreciation for their appearance with compliments or affection.
- **Sexually Pursued**: Initiate intimacy to affirm their desirability and deepen your connection.
- **Financially Appreciated**: Acknowledge their contributions to your financial stability.

Ask yourself: How well do I make my partner feel valued in these areas? Intentional effort in each can transform your relationship, making your partner feel wanted and cherished. They're worth it!

The Ultimate Guide to Loving Your Partner

To keep Jolene's favorite things front and center, I created a document to capture her preferences. It began as a simple list of her favorite flowers, foods, and hobbies but soon grew to include her clothing and jewelry sizes, travel dreams, favorite songs, and artists. I even added funny quotes she's said that make me smile. Over time, this document evolved into a detailed map for loving Jolene in specific, meaningful ways.

It's also become a relationship journal, storing itineraries from our past trips and memories we've created together. I've jokingly told Jolene that if anything happens to me, she could hand this guide to her next partner to skip years of relationship guesswork!

Create a similar document for your partner. It doesn't need to be as detailed as mine, but it can become a powerful tool to deepen your connection. Use the two Ultimate Guide templates in Part 5 to start—one for each partner—and save a digital copy to update as you learn more. This small effort can transform how you love and cherish your partner.

Loving Beyond Romance

While this chapter emphasizes romance, loving your partner in non-romantic ways is just as vital. Everyday acts of care show your partner they're valued in all seasons of life. Consider these examples:

- Picking up medication when they're bedridden with illness.
- Making popcorn for a cozy movie night at home.
- Waiting patiently in a waiting room during their medical procedure.
- Pretreating stains on their favorite shirt.
- Applying medication or ointment to hard-to-reach spots.
- Cleaning the bathroom when they're hit with a stomach bug.

Reality TV romance shows focus on arousal, desire, and excitement but rarely highlight these quieter, non-romantic acts of love. While passion fuels connection, a lasting relationship thrives on meeting everyday needs. Use tools like the Ultimate Guide from Part 5 to note your partner's practical needs alongside their romantic desires, and set calendar reminders to stay proactive. Your partner deserves your best, dig deeper to meet their needs, both big and small. They're worth it!

Mantra

We are all unique in the way we want to be loved. I'll clearly express my desires and seek to understand and meet the needs of my partner.

Chapter 16
Gifts!

"Give without remembering; receive without forgetting."
—*Diane Barton*

For some, gifts are a powerful token of affection, delighting the recipient with even the smallest present. I'm not a natural gift-giver, so this used to feel awkward. But when I realized how much gifts meant to Jolene, I decided to embrace the challenge and change my approach.

I started by noting her preferences in my Ultimate Guide document, capturing every hint about what she loves and the little things that bring her joy. With this knowledge, I shop with confidence, knowing my gifts will resonate. My past gifts were often thoughtless, but now they're intentional and heartfelt. Gift-giving has become fun for me, something I never expected to enjoy. This focus on thoughtful gifts for Jolene has also made me a better gift-giver for other loved ones. Add your partner's favorite things to your Ultimate Guide. Thoughtful giving shows your partner they're worth the effort, and you might just find joy in it too!

Cheat Sheet of Thoughtful Gift Ideas

Thoughtful gifts don't need to break the bank to make your partner feel loved. Use this list as inspiration to pick items your partner will adore. Many are affordable, and a little intention goes a long way!

- Photo Calendar
- Framed Photos
- Greeting Card
- Personalized Gifts
- Jewelry
- Lingerie
- Winter Socks
- Scarf
- Concert Tickets
- Movie Tickets
- Board or Card Games
- Soaps or Bubble Bath
- Puzzles
- Lotion
- Spa Gift Card
- Roses or Flowers
- Head Massager
- Back Scratcher
- Specialty Cupcake
- Candy Bars or Sweet Treat
- Favorite Drink
- Gift Cards

Elevating Your Gift Giving

Thoughtful gift-giving goes beyond the gift itself—presentation and delivery can make your partner feel truly special. Thoughtful presentation and delivery show your partner they're worth the effort. Enhance your gifts with these tips:

- **Wrap with Care**: Elevate the experience with wrapping paper, ribbon, or a bow. A beautifully presented gift shows effort and thoughtfulness.
- **Plan the Delivery**: How you give the gift adds to its impact. Consider these ideas:
  - » Present it during a romantic dinner date
  - » Hide it for them to find
  - » Tuck it into their pocketbook, briefcase, or backpack
  - » Arrange a surprise delivery to their workplace

> **"When you give, it comes back to you."**
> —*Mr. T*

Make it your lifelong pursuit to discover what your partner loves and surprise them with thoughtful gifts. I pity the fool who neglects this advice. Gifts don't need to be lavish—homemade cards, baked treats, or small tokens can mean just as much as store-bought presents. Gifts given with sincerity and adoration are priceless. Sprinkle your partner with love through thoughtful gestures, and watch your bond grow.

Mantra

The gifts I offer will be well planned and thoughtfully given. I'll accept gifts with gratitude and appreciation.

Chapter 17
Capturing and Preserving Memories

"Sometimes you will never know the value of a
moment until it becomes a memory."
—*Dr. Seuss*

As a child, my father insisted I write a journal entry every Sunday afternoon. I wasn't thrilled, but that journal now offers a priceless glimpse into my youth. Perhaps you kept diaries or journals growing up too. Have you considered journaling your relationship together? Documenting your shared moments can deepen your bond and create a lasting treasure. Here are some journaling ideas to try:

- **High/Low Journal**: After trips or events, Jolene and I do a "High/Low" review. We each share three highlights (highs) and one thing we didn't love (low). It's a fun way to discover what stood out to each other, and we record these to cherish later.
- **Super Special Stories**: Jot down your "greatest hits" as a couple—cherished memories, funny moments, or lessons learned. When I prepared eulogies for my grandparents, Robert and Phyllis Crooks, I collected their stories and family memories. Those few pages became a family heirloom, filled with humor and wisdom for future generations. Keep a small notebook or digital document for your own special stories, capturing precious, humorous, or wise moments.
- **Happy Book**: When I met Jolene, she suggested we each keep a "Happy Book" to note anything that brings joy, from "guacamole" to "beach walks."

Whether you prefer a high-quality notebook or a digital file, consider journaling together. Take occasional photos of physical pages to preserve them if lost or damaged. These records become a legacy of your love.

My Happy Book: A Template for Joy

Capture the moments, big and small, that bring joy to your life and relationship. Inspired by Jolene's idea, the Happy Book is a simple way to record what makes you smile, from "sipping drinks together" to "hearing your partner laugh." Use this template to start, and add entries to your Ultimate Guide for easy reference. Set a calendar reminder to revisit and update it regularly. Your partner, and your shared happiness, are worth it!

My Happy Book

Instructions: Write down anything that brings you joy—moments, things, or experiences. Add to it over time, and share with your partner to deepen your connection.

1.   11.

2.   12.

3.   13.

4.   14.

5.   15.

6.   16.

7.   17.

8.   18.

9.   19.

10.   20.

Continue adding entries as your list grows. Reflect on these with your partner to celebrate your shared joy!

Photographs and Videos

I cherish capturing our life through photos and videos. After our trips, I love creating a 'movie' with the best moments from our photographs and clips. It's such a joy to relive those sweet memories and experience them again and again.

> "A photograph can be an instant of life captured for eternity that will never cease looking back at you."
> —*Brigette Bardot*

Memories can fade quickly, but photographs, home movies, and journals bring them vividly back to life. I recently discovered 8mm films from Jolene's childhood and had them professionally digitized. Watching her parents hold her as a child was truly priceless. Though the films are silent, her deaf parents communicated through sign language, and Jolene could understand every word in those 'silent' moments—a beautiful connection to her past.

Photography Tips

1. **Mind the Lighting**: Pay attention to lighting, whether indoors or outdoors. Shoot early in the morning or during the evening to avoid harsh sunlight and capture soft, flattering tones.

2. **Check the Background**: Before snapping a photo, scan the background to avoid unwanted objects or people that could distract from your subject.

3. **Print Your Favorites**: Every few months, review your photos and select the best ones to print, preserving your memories in a tangible form.

4. **Apply the Rule of Thirds**: For dynamic compositions, try placing your subject in one-third of the frame, leaving two-thirds open to showcase the background.

5. **Use the Timer for Wider Shots**: While selfies are fun, use the camera timer to capture broader scenes, acting as your personal photographer.

6. **Offer and Request Photo Help**: Kindly offer to take photos for others—it's an appreciated gesture that often leads to reciprocal help.

7. **Vary Your Orientation**: Mix up your shots by taking photos both horizontally and vertically to add variety.

8. **Experiment with Expressions**: Smiles are timeless, but incorporate serious, silly, or candid expressions to add personality and fun to your photos.

9. **Capture Candid Moments**: While posed shots are great, candid photos often convey the most authentic emotions.

10. **Backup Regularly**: To protect your precious memories, back up your photos and videos to a cloud service (like Google Photos or iCloud) or an external drive.

Scrapbooks

Scrapbooks can range from simple photo albums to intricate collections of mementos and journal entries. Over the years, I've crafted two scrapbooks for Jolene, each one deepening our connection and creating a cherished archive of memories to relive together. Many major photo printing companies offer user-friendly tools to design and print personalized scrapbooks with your selected photos and captions. Even if you don't consider yourself creative, these services make scrapbooking a breeze.

Mementos

It's easier than ever to create mementos that celebrate your relationship with your partner. You can craft personalized puzzles, blankets, socks, and more, whether homemade or purchased. We collect unique Christmas ornaments from the places we visit, which we proudly display on our tree each year, bringing our cherished memories to life.

Decluttering Memories

As we've decluttered our home and parted with some possessions, I've held onto the memories of meaningful mementos by photographing them. When space is limited, a photo captures the essence of the object, offering nearly the same satisfaction as holding it. This allows us to let go of physical belongings while keeping their cherished memories alive.

One Last Letter

As a final gift to Jolene, I've written a heartfelt letter to say goodbye after I'm gone. In it, I pour out my love, share cherished memories, and offer closure to our deep friendship and love. I update it periodically and keep it sealed in her memento box.

I'm sentimental and a bit quirky, so this may seem unusual, but if your partner treasures love letters, they'll likely cherish this final gift. Consider including a few beloved photographs with the letter. If this idea resonates with you, consider leaving "one last letter" to other family and close friends as a sweet expression of love.

Mantra

Our history is special. I can preserve memories with journals,
words, photographs, and keepsakes. Our legacy will
gladden my heart and satisfy my spirit.

Chapter 18
Still Not Perfect

"The best thing to hold onto in life is each other."
—Audrey Hepburn

I hope the stories and perspectives in this book have inspired you to nurture your relationship in fresh and exciting ways. How much can you enhance your connection with your partner? No relationship is ever perfect—ours certainly isn't, and it never will be. We face challenges and difficulties that arise from time to time, some quite significant.

> **"When you stumble, make it part of the dance."**
> —*Unknown*

While writing this book, I hit pause several times when our relationship hit rough patches. Quarrels triggered mental blocks that stalled my progress. I only felt inspired to write about relationships when we were truly in sync. But we don't always vibe effortlessly—some days, we're just getting by.

Tough days can spark poorly timed comments, missteps, or lingering memories of past mistakes. Though perfection may not be achievable, a deeply satisfying and mutually nurturing relationship absolutely is.

When I'm weighed down by personal or relational setbacks, I turn to one of my favorite quotes for perspective:

> **"Obstacles are there to signify how bad you want something. Failure is the passageway to success. It's how you respond to failures or obstacles, or those stumbles, the brick walls that will ultimately determine your results. You can let your failures hit you square in the face and knock you out for good or you can get up and fight back. You will always pass failure on the way to success. It's about never being content with where you are at the present. Moving forward with incessant vigor to want more out of yourself. To want to do better. To have that internal fire to not end up with failure. Do you have it in you?"**
> —*Jaret Grossman*

I know I have what it takes! My relationship is worth every ounce of effort. Despite past failures, I'm still fighting for it today. If you see goodness and hope in your relationship, fight for yours too!

Mantra

My relationship may not be perfect but it will be strengthened with grace. I will live my best life and enhance my relationship forward, togetherful.

Part 2
The Relationship Roadmap 10 Pillars of Love Quiz

The Relationship Roadmap: 10 Pillars of Love

A strong, lasting relationship rests on 10 key pillars of love and commitment. When nurtured, these pillars form the foundation of an unbreakable bond. They are:

1. Trust and Honesty
2. Support and Encouragement
3. Health and Well-Being
4. Gifts and Tokens of Affection
5. Home and Family
6. Compassion and Service
7. Humor and Fun
8. Money and Finances
9. Adventure and Excitement
10. Sex and Intimacy

The Relationship Roadmap: 10 Pillars of Love Quiz

Evaluate your relationship by scoring how often you and your partner engage in the behaviors below. Add up your total score and refer to the next section to discover your Relationship Roadmap Pillars of Love rating!

3 points = All of the time

2 points = Most of the time

1 point = Some of the time

0 points = Seldom or never

Trust and Honesty

- We are honest with each other: _____
- We keep no secrets from each other: _____
- We openly share our thoughts and feelings: _____
- We clearly communicate our needs and wants: _____
- We share our location and daily details: _____

Support and Encouragement

- We share exciting news with each other first: _____
- We are each other's biggest cheerleaders: _____
- We celebrate each other's successes: _____
- We set goals and support each other in achieving them: _____
- We comfort each other during life's challenges: _____

Health and Well-Being

- We prioritize our personal health and well-being: _____
- We encourage each other's healthy lifestyle choices: _____
- We feel safe and secure in our daily lives: _____
- Our emotional and spiritual needs are usually met: _____
- We care for each other when one of us is sick: _____

Gifts and Tokens of Affection

- We surprise each other with thoughtful gifts: _____
- We exchange sentimental items: _____
- We honor holidays and special occasions: _____
- We cherish mementos and gifts from the past: _____
- We know the types of gifts our partner enjoys: _____

Home and Family

- We joyfully attend each other's family events: _____
- We share responsibilities for our home: _____
- We align on goals for our home and decor: _____
- We collaborate on home repairs and expenses: _____
- We agree on parenting practices (if applicable): _____

Compassion and Service

- We listen attentively to each other's concerns: _____
- We are there when our partner needs care: _____
- We seek ways to ease each other's burdens: _____
- We comfort each other during tough times: _____
- We understand where our partner needs support: _____

Humor and Fun

- We share funny moments with each other: ____
- We enjoy playful teasing and good times together: ____
- We pull lighthearted pranks without getting upset: ____
- We can laugh at ourselves: ____
- We make each other laugh: ____

Money and Finances

- We have enough to meet our needs: ____
- We live within our means and save for the future: ____
- We have insurance and a plan for financial challenges: ____
- We support each other's personal purchases: ____
- We each have funds for things we enjoy: ____

Adventure and Excitement

- We try new experiences together: ____
- We take trips or mini getaways together: ____
- We are spontaneous in our dates: ____
- We explore new places for each other: ____
- We plan future adventures together: ____

Sex and Intimacy

- We make time to flirt and tease intimately: ____
- We meet each other's nonsexual intimacy needs: ____
- We meet each other's sexual intimacy needs: ____
- We share what brings us pleasure: ____
- We ask what brings our partner pleasure: ____

Total Score: ____

The Relationship Roadmap: 10 Pillars of Love Score

Add up your total score from the 10 Pillars of Love Quiz to discover your Relationship Roadmap rating. Use this rating as inspiration to strengthen any pillars that need attention. Retake the quiz periodically to track your growth and celebrate your progress!

- **126–150: Love Drunk**

  You and your partner are head over heels, in sync most of the time. Your relationship is the kind others admire and aspire to!

- **101–125: Vibing**

  Your connection is rock-solid. While not perfect, your relationship often feels like it could be.

- **76–100: Heating Up**

  You share some incredible moments, but there's room to grow. You're on the right path—keep nurturing your bond to reach new heights.

- **51–75: Slightly Above Average**

  You're doing many things well, but there's space to fine-tune your relationship. A few intentional tweaks can elevate your connection.

- **26–50: Meh**

  Your relationship has a foundation, but it could use some TLC to reignite the spark. With a bit more effort, you can rise above average!

- **0–25: Room to Improve**

  The great news? There's endless potential for growth! A renewed commitment can lead to noticeable improvements.

Growing in the 10 Pillars of Love

Now that you've completed the Relationship Roadmap: 10 Pillars of Love Quiz, explore these descriptions of each pillar. Reflect on how you and your partner can nurture and strengthen each area to deepen your bond.

1. **Trust and Honesty:** Trust is the bedrock of a confident relationship. Honesty fosters this trust, creating a safe space where both partners can be open and vulnerable.

2. **Support and Encouragement**: Having a partner who cheers you on is priceless. Supporting and celebrating each other's dreams and successes builds confidence and strengthens your connection.

3. **Health and Well-Being**: Prioritizing physical, emotional, and mental health allows you to fully cherish your time together. A healthy lifestyle safeguards your future and enhances your shared joy.

4. **Gifts and Tokens of Affection**: Thoughtful gifts, big or small, weave lasting memories into your relationship. These tokens of love serve as reminders of your deep affection for each other.

5. **Home and Family**: Your home is the heart of a fulfilling relationship. Nurturing family ties and shared responsibilities creates a warm, supportive environment that enriches your life.

6. **Compassion and Service**: Showing care and grace through acts of service deepens your bond. Being there for each other in times of need builds a resilient system of love and support.

7. **Humor and Fun**: Laughter and playfulness bring joy to your relationship. Sharing lighthearted moments and finding humor together fosters positivity and closeness.

8. **Money and Finances**: Aligning on financial goals and managing money wisely reduces stress and builds stability. A shared vision for your finances brings peace today and hope for tomorrow.

9. **Adventure and Excitement**: Infusing your relationship with new experiences keeps it vibrant. Embracing adventures together sparks excitement and keeps your connection fresh and engaging.

10. **Sex and Intimacy**: A strong intimate connection guards against distance and division. Learning to meet each other's sexual and emotional needs fosters fulfillment and deepens your bond.

Part 3
The Relationship Roadmap Adventure Guide

Many of us fall into comfortable routines with our partners, letting the thrill and spontaneity of early dating days fade. A touch of adventure can breathe new life into a relationship. One date night, I shook things up by taking Jolene to a new restaurant in a nearby small town. As routine as dining out can feel, this simple change of a new town turned into a memorable evening. The city was already decked out for Christmas, with twinkling lights casting a festive glow. The crisp evening air heightened our excitement for the holiday season. Before dinner, Jolene wanted to browse a local shop, so we strolled through, admiring Christmas ornaments and soaking in the charm.

I hadn't planned to create a Hallmark-worthy moment in that quaint downtown, but it happened. By stepping outside our usual date-night routine, I gave us a fresh, joyful experience—one that required almost no effort but left us both delighted.

Are You Keeping It Fresh?

Spontaneity and small gestures can keep your relationship vibrant. Take this quick quiz to see how you and your partner are sparking excitement in your daily lives. Score your actions over the past month, then compare results to inspire each other!

I've taken my partner to a new restaurant:

0 times = 0 points   1 time = 2 points   2 or more times = 4 points

I've left my partner a note or card:

0 times = 0 points   1 time = 2 points   2 or more times = 4 points

I've bought something new or worn something attractive around my partner:

0 times = 0 points   1 time = 2 points   2 or more times = 4 points

I've taken my partner on a date night to a new place we've never been:

0 times = 0 points   1 time = 2 points   2 or more times = 4 points

Total Score:

Partner #1 _____ Partner #2 _____

0 - 3: Boring!

4 - 6: Kinda Interested!

7 - 9: Oh Wow!

10 - 12: You Totally Excite Me!

Something to Look Forward To

As a child, I eagerly awaited three moments each year: our beach trip, my birthday, and Christmas. I vividly recall spending hours poring over the toy section of the hefty Sears Christmas catalog, circling and dog-earing pages to ensure Santa knew my wishes.

We lived simply back then, and I rarely received those coveted toys. Yet, one of my fondest memories is the time spent with that catalog. The anticipation of possibly getting a toy was nearly as thrilling as unwrapping one.

I believe most of us share excitement for upcoming events or surprises. We all crave something to strive for, whether it's a big dream or just reaching the weekend. My hope is to inspire you to aim beyond simply making it to Friday and find deeper goals to fuel your enthusiasm.

> **"Pleasure is found first in anticipation, later in memory."**
> —*Gustave Flaubert*

Reflect on your calendar and consider the next six months. Is there something you're excited about? If your schedule feels empty, don't worry—there's still time to plan! Social media is a fantastic tool for planning memorable date nights. Follow venues, auditoriums, cities, and entertainment providers to stay in the loop. Subscribe to your favorite performers for early ticket sale notifications. You can also sign up for community event calendars. Our city hosts free concerts, and I'm always thrilled when their schedule drops. There's no shortage of things to do!

Make a Plan

Ready to reignite your relationship? This book is your perfect starting point. Part 4 is packed with 250+ unique date ideas to deliver adventure and connection. But inspiration alone isn't enough—you need to take action to bring these experiences to life. Thinking about it won't make it happen!

"If you are patient...and wait long enough...nothing will happen."

—Jim Davis

With a plan in place, you set your relationship up to thrive. Prioritize it by scheduling dates, setting reminders, and following through with commitment!

Date Night Selection Strategy

Jolene and I have often scheduled date nights without firm plans, which can lead to lackluster evenings at a restaurant. We've also faced disappointing dates when each of us wants to do something the other isn't excited about.

Trying new or challenging activities creates opportunities for growth. By approaching our partner's date ideas with an open mind and positive attitude, we can find joy in sharing the experience. To make this work, we need a system to blend dates each partner chooses, ensuring both feel engaged and valued.

Partner #1 _____

Date Idea List

-
-
-
-
-

Partner #2 _____

Date Idea List

-
-
-
-
-

Once you've created your lists, alternate weeks between each partner's date ideas. Approach your partner's choice with enthusiasm and an open mind, giving yourself permission to enjoy the experience. Use my self-talk phrase: "This could be fun!" Repeat it until it sinks in—this WILL be fun!

Relationship Getaways

Life's demands can strain your relationship. With work, parenting, and other responsibilities pulling you in countless directions, it's hard to fully connect. A relationship getaway offers an escape from stress, allowing you to focus on each other. Here are six distinct retreat ideas to rekindle your bond:

1. The Work Day Escape

Inspired by employees taking "mental health days," I created a unique "Work Day Escape Card" for Jolene. The card's exterior warns her to open it only when she needs an instant escape from work stress. Once opened, it triggers an immediate getaway: the partner who opens it notifies the other, and both must leave work as soon as possible (it's a "family emergency," right?). My basic card directs us to meet for a lunch date or grab takeout and head home to relax. Not every job allows the flexibility to drop everything mid-shift, but if yours does, why not enjoy a spontaneous break together?

2. The Economy Day Trip

You don't need a hotel stay to enjoy a relaxing and memorable trip. We're lucky to have mountains just an hour's drive away, with countless hikes and waterfalls to explore. Even without state or national parks nearby, a day trip can be an adventure anywhere.

One of our favorite escapes was a day trip to Marion and Old Fort in Western North Carolina. We wandered through charming downtowns, browsed a vibrant farmer's market, discovered treasures in old bookstores, and savored fresh doughnuts from a local bakery. We spent less than $50 but created memories I still cherish.

Plan your own day trip to a destination within 1–2 hours of home:

- Park and stroll the downtown area, if available.
- Visit the local Chamber of Commerce for insider tips or research online beforehand.
- Enjoy activities you love—hiking, shopping, or exploring.
- Try a new restaurant for a special meal.
- Capture the moment with photos to preserve the memories.

3. The Weekend Getaway

While grand vacations are wonderful, weekend mini retreats can be just as rejuvenating. Our favorite getaways are often just a few hours from home. One standout was a weekend at the Dirty Dancing Festival in Lake Lure, NC, only 90 minutes away. I'd never seen Dirty Dancing, so watching it for the first time on a massive outdoor screen, framed by mountains and a stunning sunset, was unforgettable. Hundreds of passionate fans sang along, having the time of their lives! Beyond the festival, we hiked to the summit of Chimney Rock State Park and to Hickory Nut Falls, played mini golf, and explored charming local shops. It was the perfect weekend escape.

Make a habit of planning 3–4 mini getaways each year. The start of a new season is a great time to schedule your next adventure. These quick trips will create lasting memories.

> **"In life, it's not where you go, it's who you travel with."**
> —*Charles Shultz*

Some of our getaways revolve around concerts or festivals, while others are open-ended, letting us discover new interests along the way. Use a local map to find destinations within driving distance and research activities and reviews to plan seasonal escapes. Though called a "weekend getaway," these trips can happen any day of the week. Midweek adventures are often cheaper and less crowded, offering a more relaxed experience.

4. The Big Trip Vacation

Our Maine road trip was one of my favorite big adventures. Over several days, we meandered from Portland to Acadia National Park, stopping whenever curiosity struck. With no rigid schedule, just the two of us, a map, and a thirst for exploration, we embraced the journey. Visiting lighthouses became a playful quest, hunting down hidden gems like the elusive Squirrel Point Lighthouse—our toughest find. Jolene even got us inside (possibly bending the rules a bit)! Those carefree days remain unforgettable.

> "May your adventures bring you closer together,
> even as they take you far away from home."
> —*Trenton Lee Stewart*

It took us years to afford bigger vacations, and that's okay. If a grand trip isn't in your budget, focus on day trips or weekend mini getaways—memorable couple's adventures don't require a big spend. When you're financially ready, consider splurging on an occasional big trip to create lasting memories.

5. The Mystery Trip

Jolene once surprised me with a mystery weekend in Arkansas, arranging flights and keeping the destination a secret. Though I was hesitant, I embraced the adventure. In Arkansas, she drove us deep into the backwoods, pulling up to a gated entrance in the middle of nowhere. I was utterly perplexed. The gate swung open, and we followed a gravel road to the stunning home and farm of P. Allen Smith. Jolene had secured tickets to tour his picturesque property and join him and other guests for a memorable dinner. The experience was unforgettable! Letting go and embracing a surprise can be thrilling. Plan a mystery trip for your partner and see if it elicits the same joy it did for me.

6. The Cruise

A cruise is unlike any vacation I've experienced—it's like an adult summer camp where you can do whatever you want, whenever you want. Maximize your trip by attending concerts, events, and comedy shows to get the full value. Falling asleep and waking up in a new, exciting port every day was thrilling. Snorkeling on a cruise excursion was a life highlight!

I had many hesitations before our first cruise, but I'm so glad I pushed past them. If you're unsure, start with a short cruise to test the waters. When I shared that I was going on my first cruise, more than one person said, "It won't be your last!" Sure enough, I booked another cruise soon after. I encourage every couple to try at least one cruise—it's an adventure you won't forget!

Fun Anywhere

A few years ago, we visited Pikeville, Kentucky, where I met one of my comic book idols, Larry Hama, at a convention. Beyond the event, the small town offered little, so we had to get creative. Eating Kentucky Fried Chicken in Kentucky brought a chuckle! We discovered a pleasant park and explored the Hatfields and McCoys history in nearby Matewan, West Virginia. The activities weren't spectacular, but they were special because of my company.

Embrace adventure with an open heart and find joy in the simplest moments. Be the person who sees every experience, big or small, as a chance to create lasting memories with those you love!

Fun Nowhere

A creative couple can transform a quiet day at home into a memorable adventure. Here are ideas to turn a mundane day into something special:

- **Movie and Popcorn Night**: Recreate the cinema experience with theater-style popcorn and cozy vibes.
- **Watch It Snow**: On a snowy morning, open the curtains, snuggle in bed, and enjoy the view. Share stories of your favorite snowy memories.
- **Board Game Battle**: Pick a game you both love and dive into some friendly competition.
- **Creative At-Home Dates**: Explore my 250+ date ideas for more ways to ellicit joy at home without leaving the house.

One Bag Travel and Packing Strategies

When planning our first UK trip, I stumbled across a quote: "There are two types of people—those who pack light and those who wish they had." Inspired, we embraced the one-bag challenge, carrying everything in a travel backpack. For 12 days, we explored the UK with just one bag each—and loved it! While other tourists dragged bulky luggage over cobblestone streets, we moved freely, hands unburdened, navigating cities with ease.

Choosing the right bag was the key to our one-bag lifestyle. After reading countless reviews, I found my ideal gear: the Patagonia Black Hole Mini MLC. Spacious enough for essentials yet compact enough to fit under an airplane seat, it's perfect. When selecting your bag, consider clamshell designs—they open fully for easy access and organization at your destination.

> **"You will at some point reach a transcendent moment,
> in which your one bag will be small and light enough to
> carry without consequence, no longer of any meaningful concern.
> And from that instant your travel experiences will be forever changed,
> with an unfettered freedom that is quite simply beyond the
> understanding of those who remain bound to baggage."**
> *—Doug Dyment*

One-bag travel requires tweaking your packing routine for success. The key shift? Pack only what you need, not what you might need. Create a strict list of essentials and stick to it. Rely on items available at your destination—most hotels and lodgings provide complimentary toiletries, hairdryers, and other essentials. For items you must pack, choose high-quality, travel-sized options.

For clothing, adopt a capsule wardrobe approach. Select versatile pieces that mix and match, allowing you to create fresh outfits from limited items. Jeans are a game-changer—they pair with nearly anything and stay fresh longer. It's perfectly fine to rewear clothes during your trip, keeping your pack light and your adventure carefree.

Laundry On the Go

For trips longer than a few days, plan to keep your clothes fresh with these laundry options:

- **Hotel and Lodging Machines**: Many accommodations offer laundry facilities or services. Check ahead to ensure your stops have machines available when needed. Pack detergent.

- **Laundromats**: In Scotland, we enjoyed lunch in a laundromat—an unusual spot, but it made washing clothes a breeze! Plan laundromat stops in your itinerary and bring detergent sheets.

- **Hand Washing**: For small loads or single items, wash by hand in a sink or dry bag with water and detergent. Knead, rinse, wring, and hang to dry. We pack single-use liquid detergent pouches for this purpose.

- **Laundry Services**: Professional laundry or dry cleaning is a pricier option. As budget-conscious travelers, we rarely use it, but it's a nice treat when convenience matters.

These strategies keep your one-bag wardrobe fresh, letting you focus on the adventure!

Clothes Packing Methods for One-Bag Travel

Packing preferences vary, so there's no one-size-fits-all method. Here are four techniques to consider for efficient, organized one-bag travel:

- **Rolling Technique**: Fold clothes neatly, then roll them tightly. This method reduces wrinkles for items like shirts and shorts. I use it at home for my dresser organization and occasionally on trips for specific pieces.

- **Flat Packing**: Fold clothes vertically and stack them flat, tailored to your bag's dimensions. This classic approach maximizes space and keeps items accessible.

- **Packing Cubes**: These zippered pouches organize clothes by category. Ideal for the organization enthusiast, they work best when sized to fit your bag.

- **Compression Packing Cubes**: Equipped with double zippers, these cubes compress clothes to save space. Note that while they reduce volume, the weight remains, so pack wisely to avoid overloading.

On my first minimalist trip, I tested each method, ultimately choosing a hybrid approach. I laid most clothes flat for efficiency, used a small compression cube for socks and underwear, and rolled a few items to fill tight spaces in my backpack. Experiment with these techniques to find what suits your travel style best.

Safety and Security While Traveling

New destinations can be thrilling, but excitement can make you forget basic safety. On our trip to London, I was swept away snapping photos of Big Ben, Tower Bridge, and the London Eye as crowds rushed by. Jolene quickly reminded me to stay vigilant, pulling me back to the safety habits we'd planned. Thieves target unprepared travelers, so here are tips to stay secure and enjoy your adventure:

- **Stay Alert in Crowds**: Watch your surroundings in busy markets or tourist spots. Look out for each other, and avoid flashing phones, purses, or wallets—thieves can snatch and run.
- **Secure Valuables**: Keep your wallet in a front pocket or use a sling bag under clothing. Pickpocketing is common but preventable with situational awareness.
- **Protect Your Vehicle**: Bring valuables (e.g., cameras, bags) into your lodging nightly to deter theft. Always lock car doors—thieves rarely break windows but will exploit unlocked doors.
- **Choose Safe Stays**: Research safer neighborhoods and pay a bit more if needed. Even in "nice" areas, stay aware of your surroundings.
- **Pick Reputable Tours**: Opt for well-reviewed guides or services, even if pricier. Saving money on sketchy excursions can cost you dearly.
- **Avoid Late Nights**: As my parents advised, "Nothing good happens after midnight." Rest in your lodging instead of wandering unfamiliar areas late at night.

- **Carry a Backup Card**: Store a spare credit card in your luggage or hotel safe. If your primary card is lost or stolen, cancel it and use the backup.

Don't let worry overshadow your trip. With basic precautions, you'll stay safe and have a blast!

Vacation Transportation Options

For years, we defaulted to renting a car at new destinations. A trip to Nashville, where our hotel's shuttle service simplified everything, opened my eyes to other possibilities. Inspired, we challenged ourselves to rely solely on public transportation and ridesharing in San Diego—and it was fantastic! We avoided the stress of driving in unfamiliar areas, searching for parking, or managing a rental car.

On our first trip to England and Scotland, we skipped car rentals entirely. Some of our fondest memories came from riding the tube, buses, boats, rideshares, and trains. These journeys let us soak in the scenery, plan adventures, and relax, turning transportation into a fun part of the experience.

Skipping car rentals is not only convenient but also saves money. In many tourist destinations, parking fees alone exceed the cost of rideshares or public transit. In St. Louis, a rideshare to the Gateway Arch was cheaper than parking and dropped us right at the park entrance!

Alternative transportation works best in cities with robust options and may not suit rural trips. Handing off driving to local transit has transformed my travel experience, making it more stress-free and enjoyable.

70+ Travel Tips and Tricks for Memorable Adventures

Travel can strengthen your bond and create lasting memories with your partner. Through trial and error, I've compiled these tips to make your trips more enjoyable, efficient, and stress-free:

1. **Packing List**: This book includes a comprehensive checklist for your adventures.
2. **Plastic Grocery Bags**: For dirty laundry, trash, or wrapping shoes to keep luggage clean.
3. **Stuff Shoes**: Maximize space by tucking socks and small items into luggage packed shoes.
4. **Empty Water Bottle**: Fill at airport water stations, avoiding overpriced drinks.
5. **Distinctive Luggage**: Use identifiable luggage or tags for quick recognition at baggage claim.
6. **Small Cooler**: Pack a cooler for car road trips to keep drinks cold or extend perishables.
7. **Arrive Early at Airports**: It's preferable to be waiting for a flight than stress about missing it.
8. **Non-Perishable Snacks**: Carry snacks to prevent "hangry" moments during travel.
9. **Record Parking Location**: Snap a photo of your parking spot at your destinations.
10. **Request Top-Floor Rooms**: Ask for a top-floor hotel room to avoid noise from above.
11. **Ear Plugs or Noise-Canceling Headphones**: Pack these for flights or noisy accommodations.
12. **Alternative Transportation**: Public transit and rideshares are often cheaper and less stressful.
13. **Avoid Sun Glare**: Avoid early eastbound morning or late westbound afternoon driving.
14. **Digital Document Backups**: Store photos of passports and insurance cards in the cloud.

15. **Monitor Flight Prices**: Track prices to secure preferred flight times and better rates.

16. **Clean Home Before Leaving**: Wash dishes and remove trash for a fresh return.

17. **Offline Maps**: Download maps for offline use or carry physical maps.

18. **Insulated Water Bottle**: Invest in a travel-sized, stainless steel bottle for sweat-free hydration.

19. **Ice Up Daily**: Fill insulated bottles with hotel ice each morning for hiking or exploring.

20. **Adjust to Time Zones**: Ignore thinking about what time it is at home to adapt more quickly.

21. **Do Your Homework**: Research destinations for must-do activities and specific places of interest.

22. **Off-Season Travel**: Visit during non-peak seasons for fewer crowds and lower rates.

23. **Car Emergency Kit**: Keep a kit with essentials for road trips in your vehicle.

24. **Carry-On Essentials**: Pack essentials in your personal item in case luggage is lost.

25. **Seek Discounts**: Find attraction and dining coupons at visitor centers, displays, and online.

26. **Always Pack a Swimsuit**: Be prepared when pools or beaches pop up unexpectedly.

27. **Carry Cash**: Bring bills and coins for small purchases, tolls, parking, or tips.

28. **Grocery Store Dining**: Save money with grocery or convenience store "meal deals."

29. **Visit Tourism Centers**: Stop by visitor centers for updated local information and services.

30. **Savor the Moment**: Slow down to fully enjoy the special places you visit.

31. **Offline Entertainment**: Download books or movies for layovers or areas without internet.

32. **Respect Wildlife**: Keep a safe distance from animals.

33. **First Aid Kit**: Pack a simple kit with medical supplies and medications.

34. **Check Reviews**: Consult multiple sources, including negative reviews of destinations.

35. **Ask Locals**: Chat with rideshare drivers or locals for insider tips on the area.

36. **Mail Hold**: Arrange for the post office or a friend to hold your mail during trips.

37. **Break In Shoes**: Wear new shoes well before travel to avoid discomfort.

38. **Double-Bag Liquids**: Use high-quality bags to secure liquids in your luggage.

39. **Embrace Positivity**: Turn mishaps into opportunities—lost luggage means new clothes.

40. **Avoid Rush Hour**: Time drives to bypass big-city traffic.

41. **Free Ice**: Top off bottles and coolers with lodging or restaurant ice to avoid buying it.

42. **Check Sunrise/Sunset Times**: Daylight can vary significantly within the same time zone.

43. **Outskirts Lodging**: Stay on the outskirts of your destination for better rates.

44. **Study Transit Maps**: Download or photograph subway/bus maps to avoid wrong routes.

45. **Travel Sunblock**: Pack a small bottle for unexpected sun exposure.

46. **Scenic Stops**: Search for interesting stops along your route for exploration and breaks.

47. **Secure Your Home**: Use alarms, cameras, or timers for lights to deter intruders while away.

48. **Extra Medications**: Pack surplus medications for unexpected trip extensions.

49. **Permanent Hygiene Kit**: Keep a travel-ready hygiene kit in your luggage for frequent trips.

50. **International Cell Service**: Arrange affordable cell service to avoid costly roaming costs.

51. **Fun Extras**: Pack a Frisbee, Waboba, or pickleball gear if space allows for spontaneous fun.

52. **Understand Currency**: Learn basic local currency for small transactions.

53. **Inspect Accommodations**: Walkthrough to ensure it meets expectations before unpacking.

54. **Wool Socks**: Pack thin-to-medium (merino or alpaca) for odor-resistant wear.

55. **Dry Wet Items**: Hang damp clothes to dry, but avoid drying on AC vents to avoid odors.

56. **Camera Timers**: Use timers for couple or group photos.

57. **Plan Ahead**: Research via videos, articles, or online communities.

58. **Book Attractions Early**: Reserve tickets for popular attractions to avoid missing out.

59. **Power Adapters**: Buy international power adapters before traveling.

60. **Schedule Downtime**: Plan rest to avoid burnout and exhaustion from overpacked itineraries.

61. **Lightweight Daypack**: My Osprey Ultralight Stuff Sack excelled for day trips and groceries.

62. **Flexible Itinerary**: Stay open to spontaneous changes, like an impromptu event you discover.

63. **Hotel Shuttles**: Use hotel shuttles for airport or attraction transfers to save money and stress.

64. **Carry Medications**: Bring prescriptions for daily outings to stay flexible.

65. **Avoid Drowsy Driving**: Pull over, swap drivers, or grab an iced drink to stay alert.

66. **Laundry Planning**: Plan laundry to travel indefinitely with just a backpack.

67. **Loyalty Points**: Collect and use hotel or airline loyalty points for savings.

68. **Concierge Luggage Storage**: Store bags at hotels to start exploring immediately.

69. **Wet Weather Gear**: Pack a lightweight rain jacket or umbrella, if the forecast demands.

70. **Early or Late Visits**: Visit attractions early morning or late afternoon for fewer crowds.

71. **White Noise Machine**: Use a travel version to block noises in unfamiliar and louder settings.

72. **Skip Unnecessary Gadgets**: Avoid bulky travel accessories that add weight without value.

73. **Secure Phone/Wallet**: Never set your phone or wallet down in crowded or tense moments.

74. **Final Room Check**: Do a "sweep" to check under beds or other spots before leaving hotels.

These tips, honed through my adventures, will help you travel light, save money, and make unforgettable memories together!

The Relationship Roadmap Adventure Guide Packing List

The Basics
- Wallet/Pocketbook
- Driver's License/ID cards/Passports
- Cash/Change
- Debit/Credit Cards
- Reservation numbers & Addresses
- Insurance Info (auto and health)

Toiletries
- Body Wash
- Shampoo & Conditioner
- Toothbrush & Paste
- Dental Floss
- Deodorant
- Hair Brush/Comb
- Haircare Products
- Hair Dryer/Curler
- Makeup
- Feminine Hygiene
- Electric Razor
- Nail Clippers
- Cotton Swabs
- Lotions & Creams
- Perfume & Cologne
- Sunscreen
- Lip Balm

Clothing
- Underwear
- Bras
- Socks
- Casual Pants
- Casual & Athletic Shorts
- T-shirts
- Skirts & Dresses
- Tights/Pantyhose
- Active & Dress Shoes
- Heels/Flats
- Hats/Visors/Toboggans
- Dressy Clothing
- Pajamas
- Sandals or Flip Flops
- Swimsuit
- Sweatshirt/Hoodie
- Jacket
- Watch

Miscellaneous
- Bags (zip bags/grocery/trash)
- Beach Towels
- Clothespin Clip
- Earplugs
- Insect Repellent
- Umbrella

Medical & Medication
- Acetaminophen
- Antihistamine
- Anti-Fungal Ointment
- Bandages
- Clippers/Tweezers
- Glasses/Contacts
- Lip Balm
- Prescriptions (+extra)
- Motion Sickness Medication
- Stomach Relief
- Tissues
- Triple Antibiotic Ointment
- Vitamins & Supplements
- Wet Wipes

Entertainment
- Phone Chargers
- Earbuds or Noise-Canceling Headphones
- White Noise Machine
- Maps
- Music
- TV & Movies
- Books & Magazines

The Relationship Roadmap Adventure Guide Minimalist Packing List

I prefer a 30L or less clamshell backpack for the smoothest of minimalist travel. Focus on essentials and pack light to keep your journey stress-free and memorable.

The Basics
- Wallet/Pocketbook
- Driver's License/ID cards/Passport
- Cash/Change
- Debit/Credit Cards
- Reservation Numbers & Addresses
- Insurance Info (auto and health)

Toiletries (opt for travel-size, rely on hotel amenities when possible)
- Toothbrush & Paste
- Deodorant
- Hair Brush/Comb
- Minimal Makeup
- Minimal Feminine Hygiene
- Nail Clippers
- Sunscreen (small bottle)
- Lip Balm

Clothing (capsule wardrobe: 5–6 items, mix-and-match)
- 3 Underwear
- 1–2 Bras
- 3 Socks
- 1 Pair of Jeans
- 1 Pair Shorts/Leggings
- 2 Tops (1 T-shirt, 1 long-sleeve, neutral colors)
- 1 Pair Shoes
- 1 Swimsuit
- 1 Light Jacket or Pullover

Miscellaneous (You may or may not need)
- Reusable Water Bottle
- Plastic Bags
- Towel
- Wash or Dry Bag & Detergent Sheets
- Travel Clothesline
- Umbrella or Rain Jacket

Medical & Medication
- Small First Aid Kit:
  - Bandages
  - Antibiotic Ointment
  - Aspirin
  - Antihistamine
  - Motion Sickness/ Stomach Relief
  - Prescription Medications
  - Vitamins & Supplements

Entertainment
- Phone/Camera & Charger
- Earbuds or Noise-Canceling Headphones
- Small Journal & Pen
- Downloaded Maps, Books, or Movies
- Mini White Noise Machine

The Relationship Roadmap Camping Packing Checklist

While you won't need everything listed, be sure to consider your personal needs. Your preparation will pay off with greater comfort in the wild.

Clothing

- Pants
- Raingear
- Sandals/Flip Flops
- Shirts
- Shorts
- Swimsuit
- Shoes
- Socks
- Sunglasses
- Coats/Jackets
- Hat
- Underwear

Medical/Health

- Prescription Medications
- Emergency Medical Kit
- Eyeglasses or Contacts
- Insect Repellent
- Lip Balm

Food & Water

- Cooler
- Potable Water
- Water Purification Devices
- Food
- Snacks
- Cookware & Utensils
- Can Opener
- Knives
- Utensils
- Plates & Bowls
- Cups

Shelter

- Tent
- Tarp
- Mosquito Net
- Hammock
- Sleeping Bag
- Sheet
- Pillow
- Cot/Pad/Mattress

Hygiene

- Body Wash
- Shampoo
- Hand Sanitizer
- Brushes/Comb
- Toothbrush & Paste
- Toilet Paper
- Towels
- Wet Wipes

Miscellaneous

- Pocket Knife
- Camp Ax
- Camp Shovel
- Clothesline/Pins
- Dry Bag
- Earplugs
- Fire Starters
- Flashlights & Lanterns
- Paracord or Rope
- Maps
- Sunscreen
- Portable Table
- Plastic Bags
- Camp Chair
- Entertainment

Camping Tips and Tricks

- Don't trust the weather ratings on sleeping bags. Degrees shown are for survival, not comfort.
- Half the number of any tent sleep capacity for comfort. (e.g., a 4-person is comfortable for 2.)
- Store foodstuffs outside the campsite to avoid attracting wildlife.
- Notify loved ones of your whereabouts and plans for safety in case of an emergency.
- Carry physical copies of maps in case of phone issues.
- Don't unroll the sleeping bag until right before sleep to avoid dampness.
- Bring shoes or boots into your tent or cover them to keep them dry overnight.
- Individually wrap changes of clothes in plastic bags to keep them fresh and dry.
- Purchase brightly colored camping gear to avoid losing it in the wild.
- Bring tinder (dryer lint, paper, small sticks & twigs), kindling (bigger sticks & twigs), and dry firewood to make fire starting a breeze.

Hiking Tips

I can't tell you how many times I've been on a "gingerly" hike and regretted not bringing a small pack. My usual regret is not having water, but there are a few other items that will make your hike comfortable, safe, and enjoyable. This list can be personalized for your unique needs.

The Relationship Roadmap Hiking Day Pack Checklist

Customize the checklist to suit your specific needs, such as adding a compass or extra layers for comfort and safety.

- Water
- Snacks
- Map
- Simple Medical Kit
- Phone
- Lip Balm

The Togetherful 50 States Challenge

Many couples have a goal to visit all 50 states. We have a wooden map of the United States that my daughter created. We put pins into each state as we visit them. Use this checklist and check your ranking!

- ☐ Alabama
- ☐ Alaska
- ☐ Arizona
- ☐ Arkansas
- ☐ California
- ☐ Colorado
- ☐ Connecticut
- ☐ Delaware
- ☐ Florida
- ☐ Georgia
- ☐ Hawaii
- ☐ Idaho
- ☐ Illinois
- ☐ Indiana
- ☐ Iowa
- ☐ Kansas
- ☐ Kentucky

- ☐ Louisiana
- ☐ Maine
- ☐ Maryland
- ☐ Massachusetts
- ☐ Michigan
- ☐ Minnesota
- ☐ Mississippi
- ☐ Missouri
- ☐ Montana
- ☐ Nebraska
- ☐ Nevada
- ☐ New Hampshire
- ☐ New Jersey
- ☐ New Mexico
- ☐ New York
- ☐ North Carolina
- ☐ North Dakota

- ☐ Ohio
- ☐ Oklahoma
- ☐ Oregon
- ☐ Pennsylvania
- ☐ Rhode Island
- ☐ South Carolina
- ☐ South Dakota
- ☐ Tennessee
- ☐ Texas
- ☐ Utah
- ☐ Vermont
- ☐ Virginia
- ☐ Washington
- ☐ West Virginia
- ☐ Wisconsin
- ☐ Wyoming

The 50 States Challenge Rank and Title!

Count a point for every state you have visited. Tally your score to determine your rank and title!

- 1: Uhm… you don't get out much, do you?
- 2 - 5: Small Roadtrip Pals!
- 6 - 10: Extended Range Rovers!
- 10 - 20: Bag Packing Duo!
- 21 - 30: Getaround Gang!
- 31 - 40: Cross Country Legends!
- 41 - 49: Continental Wonders!
- 50: Solid Gold Elite Travelers! USA Complete!

The Togetherful National Parks Challenge

More ambitious than the 50 States Challenge is the National Parks Challenge. If this isn't possible, an alternative goal is to visit at least one National Park in each state.

Alaska
- ☐ Denali
- ☐ Gates of the Arctic
- ☐ Glacier Bay
- ☐ Katami
- ☐ Kenai Fjords
- ☐ Kobuk Valley
- ☐ Lake Clark
- ☐ Wrangell-St Elias

Arizona
- ☐ Grand Canyon
- ☐ Petrified Forest
- ☐ Saguaro

Arkansas
- ☐ Hot Springs

California
- ☐ Channel Islands
- ☐ Death Valley
- ☐ Joshua Tree
- ☐ Kings Canyon
- ☐ Lassen Volcanic
- ☐ Redwood
- ☐ Sequoia
- ☐ Yosemite

Colorado
- ☐ Black Canyon of Gunnison
- ☐ Great Sand Dunes
- ☐ Mesa Verde
- ☐ Rocky Mountain

Florida
- ☐ Biscayne
- ☐ Dry Tortugas
- ☐ Everglades

Hawaii
- ☐ Haleakala
- ☐ Hawaii Volcanoes

Indiana
- ☐ Indiana Dunes

Kentucky
- ☐ Mammoth Cave

Maine
- ☐ Acadia

Michigan
- ☐ Isle Royale

Minnesota
- ☐ Voyageurs

Missouri
- ☐ Gateway Arch

Montana
- ☐ Glacier

Nevada
- ☐ Great Basin

New Mexico
- ☐ Carlsbad Caverns
- ☐ White Sands

North Dakota
- ☐ Theodore Roosevelt

Ohio
- ☐ Cuyahoga Valley

Oregon
- ☐ Crater Lake

South Carolina
- ☐ Congaree

South Dakota
- ☐ Badlands
- ☐ Wind Cave

Tennessee
- ☐ Great Smoky Mountains

Texas
- ☐ Big Bend
- ☐ Guadalupe Mountains

Utah
- ☐ Arches
- ☐ Bryce Canyon
- ☐ Capitol Reef
- ☐ Canyonlands
- ☐ Zion

Virginia
- ☐ Shenandoah

Washington
- ☐ Mount Rainier
- ☐ North Cascades
- ☐ Olympic

West Virginia
- ☐ New River Gorge

Wyoming
- ☐ Grand Teton
- ☐ Yellowstone

United States Territories
- ☐ American Samoa
- ☐ Virgin Islands

The National Parks Challenge Rank and Title!

Count a point for every National Park you have visited. Tally your score to determine your National Parks Challenge Rank and Title! Your title awaits!

- 1: Ummm?
- 2 - 5: Map Merrimenters!
- 6 - 10: Backpacking Buddies!
- 10 - 20: Occupiers of the Outdoors!
- 21 - 30: Waterfall Wondercouple!
- 31 - 40: Nautical Navigators!
- 41 - 50: Wanderers of the Woodlands!
- 51 - 55: National Park Nuts!
- 56 or more: Overlords of the National Park Kingdom!

Part 4
The Relationship Roadmap 250+ Date Adventures

The Relationship Roadmap 250+ Date Adventures

This is an extensive collection of over 250 dates, ranging from thrilling and romantic to a few that are delightfully silly. Step outside your comfort zone to bring variety and excitement back into your relationship. After reviewing and checking off the dates you've completed, tally the total to determine your The Relationship Roadmap Dating Adventure Score and Official Title!

The Relationship Roadmap 250+ Date Adventures Checklist

☐ 1. 3D Movie Date
☐ 2. Allnight Date
☐ 3. Alpine Coaster Date
☐ 4. Amusement Park Date
☐ 5. Antique Shopping Date
☐ 6. Aquarium Date
☐ 7. Art Museum Date
☐ 8. Artistic Masterpiece Date
☐ 9. Auctioneering Date
☐ 10. Aviation Museum Date
☐ 11. Axe Throwing Date
☐ 12. Backyard Cookout Date
☐ 13. Baking Bread Date
☐ 14. Banana Split Date
☐ 15. Barn, Ballroom, and Dance Date
☐ 16. Batting Cages Date
☐ 17. Be in a Movie Date
☐ 18. Bike a Greenway Date
☐ 19. Billiards Date
☐ 20. Binge TV Date
☐ 21. Bingo Date
☐ 22. Blind Map Date
☐ 23. Bonfire and S'mores Date
☐ 24. Book Club Date
☐ 25. Book Lovers Date
☐ 26. Bookmark Creation Date
☐ 27. Botanical Garden Date
☐ 28. Boudoir Photo Shoot Date
☐ 29. Bowling Alley Date
☐ 30. Breakfast Club Date
☐ 31. Building Block Creations Date
☐ 32. Bubble Bath or Shower Date
☐ 33. Bucket List Date
☐ 34. Cake Date
☐ 35. Calendar Coordination Date
☐ 36. Car Show Date
☐ 37. Carriage Ride Date
☐ 38. Carnival or Fair Date
☐ 39. Casino Night Date
☐ 40. Celebrity Meet and Greet Date
☐ 41. Charcuterie Board Date
☐ 42. Chili Cookoff Date
☐ 43. Christmas Lights Date
☐ 44. City Tour Date
☐ 45. Clean Out Closet Date
☐ 46. Climbing or Repelling Date
☐ 47. Cloud Watching Date
☐ 48. Collectibles Convention Date

- [ ] 49. Comedy Club or Show Date
- [ ] 50. Concert Date
- [ ] 51. Cooking Class Date
- [ ] 52. Cool in the Pool Date
- [ ] 53. Corn Maze Date
- [ ] 54. Cornhole Tailgate Date
- [ ] 55. Couples Happy Book Date
- [ ] 56. Court Date
- [ ] 57. Cozy Cabin Date
- [ ] 58. Crash an Event Date
- [ ] 59. Crochet, Knit, Sew, or Stitch Date
- [ ] 60. Dance Lesson Date
- [ ] 61. Dating Profile Blind Date
- [ ] 62. Disc Golf Date
- [ ] 63. DIY Woodworking Date
- [ ] 64. Double Date Date
- [ ] 65. Draw Me, Draw Us Date
- [ ] 66. Drawing and Coloring Date
- [ ] 67. Drive-In Theater Date
- [ ] 68. Emergency Kit Date
- [ ] 69. Escape Room Date
- [ ] 70. Factory Tour Date
- [ ] 71. Fallen Leaves Date
- [ ] 72. Fantasy Shop Date
- [ ] 73. Fantasy Sports Draft Date
- [ ] 74. Farmers Market Date
- [ ] 75. Ferry Ride Date
- [ ] 76. Film a Commercial Date
- [ ] 77. Fireflies Date
- [ ] 78. Fireworks Viewing Date
- [ ] 79. First Impressions Date
- [ ] 80. FirstAid/CPR Date

- [ ] 81. Fishing Date
- [ ] 82. Five Love Languages Date
- [ ] 83. Flirty First Date
- [ ] 84. Food Truck Fun Date
- [ ] 85. Fort Building Date
- [ ] 86. Front Row Seats Date
- [ ] 87. Fun Dance Date
- [ ] 88. Game Night at Home Date
- [ ] 89. Gardening Class Date
- [ ] 90. Genealogy Date
- [ ] 91. Geocaching Date
- [ ] 92. Get Fit Date
- [ ] 93. Gift Exchange Date
- [ ] 94. Gingerbread House Date
- [ ] 95. Golf Driving Range Date
- [ ] 96. Go Karts Race Date
- [ ] 97. Grocery Shopping Date
- [ ] 98. Hammock Day Dream Date
- [ ] 99. Haunted House Date
- [ ] 100. Helicopter Excursion Date
- [ ] 101. Hide and Seek Date
- [ ] 102. Hike Date
- [ ] 103. Historic Downtown Date
- [ ] 104. Historic Reenactment Date
- [ ] 105. History Museum Date
- [ ] 106. Homemade Ice Cream Date
- [ ] 107. Horseback Trail Date
- [ ] 108. Hot Air Balloon Launch Date
- [ ] 109. Ice Skating Date
- [ ] 110. Jigsaw Puzzle Date
- [ ] 111. Jewelry Crafting Date
- [ ] 112. Karaoke Date

- [ ] 113. Kayaking Date
- [ ] 114. Kite Flying Fun Date
- [ ] 115. Kissology Date
- [ ] 116. LARPing Date
- [ ] 117. Laser Tag Date
- [ ] 118. Last Minute Trip Date
- [ ] 119. Letter and Postcard Date
- [ ] 120. Lighthouse Hunt Date
- [ ] 121. Limo Fancy Date
- [ ] 122. Line Dance Date
- [ ] 123. Love Soundtrack Date
- [ ] 124. Manicure Pedicure Date
- [ ] 125. Marathon Date
- [ ] 126. Massage at Home Date
- [ ] 127. Mechanical Bull Riding Date
- [ ] 128. Meetaversary Date
- [ ] 129. Memory Lane Date
- [ ] 130. Metal Detector Treasure Date
- [ ] 131. Midnight Eats Date
- [ ] 132. Mini Golf Date
- [ ] 133. Minute to Win It Date
- [ ] 134. Mission Statement Date
- [ ] 135. Model Construction Date
- [ ] 136. Movie Location Date
- [ ] 137. Movie Night at Home Date
- [ ] 138. Movie Roulette Date
- [ ] 139. Movies in the Park Date
- [ ] 140. Murder Mystery Date
- [ ] 141. Music Festival Date
- [ ] 142. Musical Talent Date
- [ ] 143. Mystical Future Date
- [ ] 144. Magicians Date
- [ ] 145. My Hometown Date
- [ ] 146. Mystery Concert Date
- [ ] 147. Mystery Location Date
- [ ] 148. Mystery Order Restaurant Date
- [ ] 149. National Park Date
- [ ] 150. Nature Nerds Date
- [ ] 151. Nature Walk Date
- [ ] 152. New Hairdo Date
- [ ] 153. New Perfume and Cologne Date
- [ ] 154. New Years Resolution & Dinner
- [ ] 155. Obstacle Course Date
- [ ] 156. Odd Festival Date
- [ ] 157. Oddball Sports Date
- [ ] 158. Olympics Day Date
- [ ] 159. Orchard or Berry Patch Date
- [ ] 160. Ornament Creation Date
- [ ] 161. Paddle Boat Date
- [ ] 162. Paintball or Airsoft Date
- [ ] 163. Paper and Origami Date
- [ ] 164. Park and Make-Out Date
- [ ] 165. Passport Date
- [ ] 166. Perfume and Cologne Night
- [ ] 167. Petting Zoo Date
- [ ] 168. Photo Shoot Date
- [ ] 169. Pickleball Date
- [ ] 170. Picnic at a Park Date
- [ ] 171. Pizzeria at Home Date
- [ ] 172. Play Dress Up Date
- [ ] 173. Playground Pals Date
- [ ] 174. Playing in the Rain Date
- [ ] 175. Poetry Date
- [ ] 176. Pottery Date

- [ ] 177. Progressive Dinner Date
- [ ] 178. Public Transportation Date
- [ ] 179. Pumpkin Carving Date
- [ ] 180. Pumpkin Patch Date
- [ ] 181. Quilt Square Trail Drive Date
- [ ] 182. RC Cars, Planes, or Boats Date
- [ ] 183. Record Player Retro Date
- [ ] 184. Re-enact Vintage Photos Date
- [ ] 185. Renaissance Festivals Date
- [ ] 186. Retro Arcade Date
- [ ] 187. River Boat Cruise Date
- [ ] 188. River Rafting Date
- [ ] 189. River Tubing Date
- [ ] 190. Roadside Attraction Date:
- [ ] 191. Rodeo Date
- [ ] 192. Rock, Gem, and Gold Date
- [ ] 193. Rock Art Date
- [ ] 194. Roller Skating Date
- [ ] 195. Romantic Fireplace Date
- [ ] 196. Ropes Course Date
- [ ] 197. Run/Walk/Jog a 5K Date
- [ ] 198. Sand Castle Date
- [ ] 199. Sand Dunes Date
- [ ] 200. Scavenger Hunt Date
- [ ] 201. Science Experiment Date
- [ ] 202. Science Museum Date
- [ ] 203. Seashell & Seaglass Hunt Date
- [ ] 204. Second Chance Prom Date
- [ ] 205. Second First Date Date
- [ ] 206. Self-Defense Class Date
- [ ] 207. Sensory Date
- [ ] 208. Sign Language Date
- [ ] 209. Skiing or Tubing Date
- [ ] 210. Skydiving Date
- [ ] 211. Sleep on the Beach Date
- [ ] 212. Snorkeling or Scuba Date
- [ ] 213. Snowman Date
- [ ] 214. Snow Much Fun Date
- [ ] 215. Solar Eclipse Date
- [ ] 216. Space View Date
- [ ] 217. Special Event Date
- [ ] 218. Speedway Date
- [ ] 219. Sporting Event Date
- [ ] 220. Spring Clean Date
- [ ] 221. Stand Up Comedy Date
- [ ] 222. Stargazing Date
- [ ] 223. State Park Date
- [ ] 224. Stay in Bed Date
- [ ] 225. Sunday Afternoon Drive Date
- [ ] 226. Sunrise or Sunset Date
- [ ] 227. Surf, Skim, Body Board Date
- [ ] 228. Symphony or Orchestra Date
- [ ] 229. Tacky Thrift Store Date
- [ ] 230. Tandem Bike Ride Date
- [ ] 231. Taste Test Date
- [ ] 232. Technology Free Date
- [ ] 233. Tennis Date
- [ ] 234. Tent Camping Date
- [ ] 235. Theater, Drama, or Play Date
- [ ] 236. Time Capsule Date
- [ ] 237. Tourist Trap Date
- [ ] 238. Train Ride Date
- [ ] 239. Trampoline Park Date
- [ ] 240. Trivia Night Date

- ☐ 241. Try a New Restaurant Date
- ☐ 242. Ultimate Guide Date
- ☐ 243. Valentine's Day Date
- ☐ 244. Vacation Planning Date
- ☐ 245. Video Game Date
- ☐ 246. Volunteer your Talent Date
- ☐ 247. Water Fun at Home Date
- ☐ 248. Water Park Fun Date
- ☐ 249. Waterfall Hikes Date
- ☐ 250. Wild West Date
- ☐ 251. Winter Hike Date
- ☐ 252. Wreath Creating Date
- ☐ 253. Wrestling Date
- ☐ 254. Yoga/Mindfulness Date
- ☐ 255. Zip Lining Date
- ☐ 256. Zoo Date

The Relationship Roadmap 250+ Date Adventures Descriptions

1. 3D Movie Date | Inexpensive to Moderate

Buy or borrow a 3D movie with glasses and enjoy a unique date night at home. Theaters also show 3D and 4D movies on occasion.

2. Allnight Date | Free or Inexpensive

Stay up all night and experience the twilight hours in splendor. This is easier in spots like Las Vegas or a cruise where the entertainment never stops. You may need the next date to recuperate!

3. Alpine Coaster Date | Inexpensive to Moderate

A single-seat coaster that propels you through twists and turns. You'll love hearing each other squeal in delight as you work your way around the course.

4. Amusement Park Date | Moderate to Pricey

The excitement and fear of a roller coaster can bond you as you reach out to your partner in laughter. Even the lower thrill couples can find rides and shows to share.

5. Antique Shopping Date | Free or Inexpensive

I collect 1930s-60s postcards so I enjoy sifting through vintage stuff. A trip to an antique shop is a time machine. Share memories with each other as you pass by sentimental items.

6. Aquarium Date | Inexpensive to Moderate
While some science museums host small aquariums, full-fledged aquariums can be a sight to behold. Most aquariums are dark and peaceful, adding to the charm.

7. Art Museum Date | Inexpensive to Moderate
Get cultured at an art museum while admiring the different styles of art. Share with each other the ones you enjoy most.

8. Artistic Masterpiece Date | Inexpensive to Moderate
Channel your inner Bob Ross and create works of art. Choose the same subject or create two different masterpieces.

9. Auctioneering Date | Inexpensive to Moderate
When we first got married, we went to an auction and purchased bedding for cheap. Auctions can be fun to watch even if buying nothing. Who knows what treasures you might find?

10. Aviation Museum Date | Free or Inexpensive
Aviation museums are an affordable, educational date. Many are free or ask for donations. Our local museum in Hickory even has a retired F-14 Tomcat as made famous by *Top Gun*.

11. Axe Throwing Date | Inexpensive to Moderate
Rooting or competing against each other makes for a fun date. Most axe throwing venues have other activities available so you can expand the date with darts, billiards, and more.

12. Backyard Cookout Date | Inexpensive to Moderate
Prep and enjoy a cookout together. This perfect group date activity promotes discussion and relaxation over your favorite grilled goodies.

13. Baking Bread Date | Free or Inexpensive
This date heats up the kitchen as you bake your own bread. There are few things better than oven fresh bread covered in butter and honey!

14. Banana Split Date | Inexpensive to Moderate

Gather your favorite toppings and create your perfect masterpiece. You can also find a classic diner that serves these sweet treats to share.

15. Barn, Ballroom, and Dance Date | Inexpensive to Moderate

Many venues offer a beginners lesson before many dances. You don't have to be skilled to have a good time. Put yourself out there, you'll do great!

16. Batting Cages Date | Inexpensive to Moderate

These usually have adjusted speeds to accommodate new and experienced batters. Prepare to feel silly as you miss and proud when you launch one.

17. Be in a Movie Date | Free to Inexpensive

Production companies always need extras for TV shows and movies. Spend a day together on set! No previous experience is required. As a bonus, you'll get paid! Lights, camera, action!

18. Bike a Greenway Date | Free to Inexpensive

Many towns have greenways and public trails that welcome bikers. If you don't already own a bike, rent one for an enjoyable date on the trails.

19. Billiards Date | Free to Inexpensive

The billiard table is a great place for light-hearted competition and relaxed conversation. This is a fun hobby often found at arcades, community centers, and bowling alleys.

20. Binge TV Date | Free to Inexpensive

Block out a day and choose a show that you both want to binge. After collecting snacks and goodies, get comfy and binge away.

21. Bingo Date | Inexpensive to Moderate

Play Bingo! Local venues, fairs, cruises, and even casinos offer Bingo. You may win cash and prizes but you will enjoy a fun natured time.

22. Blind Map Date | Inexpensive to Moderate

Take a map of your state and cut it into squares. Place the squares in a bag and pull one out. You now have a new area to spend a day. Too ambitious? Do the same thing with a local map.

23. Bonfire and S'mores Date | Free to Inexpensive

We had a bonfire with friends and enjoyed telling stories and making s'mores. The flicker of the fire cultivates transparency, honesty, and laughter. Use oak, ash, or beech wood to enjoy a less smoky fire.

24. Book Club Date | Free to Inexpensive

Read a favorite short story to each other. The more daring may want to read and discuss an entire book together.

25. Book Lovers Date | Free to Inexpensive

Take a trip to a bookstore or a local library. I'll never forget going to a quaint used bookstore in Little Switzerland, NC.

26. Bookmark Creation Date | Free to Inexpensive

Cut cardstock into bookmark-sized strips and make your own bookmarks. Jazz up your bookmarks with cool art, colors, or words of inspiration. Consider creating a second bookmark to gift to each other.

27. Botanical Garden Date | Free to Inexpensive

Visit a botanical garden and enjoy the seasonal vegetation. I am always amazed at just how many varieties of plants there are and always see something new.

28. Boudoir Photo Shoot Date | Free to Inexpensive

If you are in a trusting and long-term relationship, take intimate photos for each other. This can be incredibly bonding if done appropriately.

29. Bowling Alley Date | Inexpensive to Moderate

Bowling is a fun date in any weather. Many bowling centers also have arcades, billiards, and air hockey so this date keeps on giving!

30. Breakfast Club Date | Inexpensive to Moderate
When was the last time you went out for breakfast? Get up for this nourishing early morning date. We don't do this often but we have a few special breakfast spots.

31. Building Block Creations Date | Inexpensive to Moderate
Purchase a building set and lose yourself in playful construction. Purchase a themed set you both love or just a box of random blocks. Simple silly dates can be some of the best.

32. Bubble Bath or Shower Date | Free or Inexpensive
If you have a tub big enough, have a warm bubble bath together. Relax and enjoy each other in a whole new setting! Alternately, enjoy the connectedness of a shower together.

33. Bucket List Date | Free or Inexpensive
List and discuss over a nice dinner what you want to see and do during your life. Remember to add items you want to accomplish or do individually and as a couple.

34. Cake Date | Free or Inexpensive
Bake and decorate a cake together. Watch a baking show and enjoy your cake with a glass of cold milk or preferred beverage.

35. Calendar Coordination Date | Free or Inexpensive
Open each of your calendars up and review the upcoming events to assure you each are on the same page with appointments, leave requests, vacations. Do it add a relaxed restaurant for greater enjoyment.

36. Car Show Date | Free or Inexpensive
You don't have to be a fan of hot rods to enjoy a car show. This is often free and usually has food vendors. If you are interested in automobiles, you'll love the camaraderie of like-minded car enthusiasts.

37. Carriage Ride Date | Inexpensive to Moderate

Is there anything more romantic than a horse pulled carriage ride? We did this once on a chilly rainy night enjoying the clopping horse hooves while cuddling under a blanket.

38. Carnival or Fair Date | Inexpensive to Moderate

A classic movie date. Stroll the venue with a bag of cotton candy or other fair foods. The Ferris wheel is the iconic heart of this date!

39. Casino Night Date | Free or Inexpensive

With a simple deck of cards, create an evening of fun playing Poker, Blackjack, or Rummy (my favorite). For added fun, play Dean Martin or turn on *Ocean's Eleven* in the background.

40. Celebrity Meet and Greet Date | Moderate to Pricey

We've based several dates around meeting Dale Murphy, P. Allen Smith, and Gary Chapman. Our interactions were brief with a few words shared before a customary photo.

41. Charcuterie Board Date | Inexpensive to Moderate

This makes for a relaxing date talking and sampling new meats, cheeses, and other goodies. Another date paired well with friends.

42. Chili Cookoff Date | Inexpensive to Moderate

Each of you make your favorite chili and invite friends or family over to do a blind taste test to see who is the blue ribbon chili winner of your relationship!

43. Christmas Lights Date | Free or Inexpensive

Inspired by *National Lampoon's Christmas Vacation*, more people than ever put on dazzling light shows! We traditionally visit an ice cream parlor after our annual Christmas lights date.

44. City Tour Date | Inexpensive to Moderate

When we were in Mount Airy, the town that inspired Mayberry in *The Andy Griffith Show*, we actually took a tour in a vintage squad car! Other ideas include bikes, trolleys, fun buses.

45. Clean Out Closet Date | Free or Inexpensive

Empty your closet, purge, and reorganize. Try on old clothes and help each other decide to keep or discard them.

46. Climbing, or Repelling Date | Free to Inexpensive

I loved bouldering "Devil's Cellar" in Table Rock, NC as we worked our way up the crevasse. For the more ambitious, try traditional rock climbing or repelling. As with all higher adventure dates, be safe and stay within your experience range. Climbing facilities are also an option.

47. Cloud Watching Date | Free or Inexpensive

Lay outside and enjoy the serene beauty of the clouds. Share what you think they look like as they float across the sky. Cirrus or cumulus clouds are generally the best.

48. Collectibles Convention Date | Inexpensive to Moderate

Even if you don't buy anything, the price of admission is worth it to walk through a vintage museum of your childhood and pop culture.

49. Comedy Club or Show Date | Inexpensive to Moderate

Sharing laughter is a great way to connect. Can't get to a live show? Find one online. I love the comedy of Kevin James, Michael Jr., and Rodney Dangerfield!

50. Concert Date | Moderate to Pricey

Choose a concert you'll both enjoy and listen to live music together. In recent years, I have loved tribute bands.

51. Cooking Class Date | Inexpensive to Moderate

Learning a new kitchen skill can be bonding and beneficial for years to come. Sign up for a class or alternatively watch a cooking show and try the techniques and recipes demonstrated. Bon appetit!

52. Cool in the Pool Date | Inexpensive to Moderate

Swim together in a private or public swimming pool. Make a day of it with snacks, drinks, and sunblock.

53. Corn Maze Date | Inexpensive to Moderate
Some have maps that you complete, while others leave you wandering. Bring a flashlight if going at night. Emerge victorious from the maze!

54. Cornhole Tailgate Date | Inexpensive to Moderate
Cornhole has become one of the great American tailgate sports. Add a burger and beverage to make this date even better!

55. Couples Happy Book Date | Free or Inexpensive
A happy book is a journal or list of things that bring you joy and happiness. Make your list together. This is a great activity to do over and over throughout your life. I do this weekly.

56. Court Date | Free or Inexpensive
Watching a public court session can be educational and informative. Not feeling a courtroom? Watch a courtroom drama.

57. Cozy Cabin Date | Moderate to Pricey
Curling up in a cabin is a romantic and delightful date. Bring games, puzzles, and snacks! Limit the use of electronics for greater connection.

58. Crash an Event Date | Free or Inexpensive
I once offered my sister, Amy, all the money in my wallet if she snuck into Hickory's annual Christmas Parade. Ten minutes later, she was walking with the parade, waving at the crowd. As a couple, politely infiltrate a party, parade, or even a wedding.

59. Crochet, Knit, Sew, or Stitch Date | Free or Inexpensive
While working at an adult day program, I spent time in the quilting room with the ladies. I learned that conversation was as important as quilting. Find a project and sew up your relationship in new ways!

60. Dance Lesson Date | Inexpensive to Moderate
Take a dance lesson together. Learning a few dances will open up future opportunities to bond. These do not need to be extensive and some events even offer free instruction.

61. Dating Profile Blind Date | Free or Inexpensive
Complete the dating profile and conversation starters at the end of this book. Bring your completed profiles to share on a "blind date" at a restaurant or venue. Dress to impress and really treat it as a blind first date. If the date goes well, maybe they can follow you home!

62. Disc Golf Date | Free or Inexpensive
Many public parks have free disc golf courses. Throw your disc at a basket in the fewest amount of throws as you compete.

63. DIY Woodworking Date | Inexpensive to Moderate
Wooden craft stores allow patrons to make functional items and decorative art for their home. Alternatively whittle or woodcarve a creation of your choice.

64. Double Date Date | Free or Inexpensive
Invite another couple on one of the 249 date night ideas or come up with your own. Building relationships with new friends adds variety to your date nights.

65. Draw Me, Draw Us Date | Free or Inexpensive
Get quality drawing paper and instruments and draw a portrait of the other person or both of you. Add colors to help the art "pop." Caricatures are fun too!

66. Drawing and Coloring Date | Free or Inexpensive
Sit down with your partner, coloring utensils, and coloring books. Pair it with classic cartoons for a real nostalgia trip.

67. Drive-In Theater Date | Inexpensive to Moderate
If you are old enough to remember drive-ins, it'll be a reminiscent experience but first timers will enjoy the unique viewing experience too!

68. Emergency Kit Date | Inexpensive to Moderate
Work together to inventory and put together an emergency kit. Continue the date by shopping for items. Celebrate your preparedness with a meal out.

69. Escape Room Date | Inexpensive to Moderate

Mystery and puzzle fans will enjoy a trip to an Escape Room. This is another great group date.

70. Factory Tour Date | Free to Inexpensive

Visit a factory and see how products are made. We've visited the Bush's Beans and the Louisville Slugger factories. Many tours offer samples.

71. Fallen Leaves Date | Free or Inexpensive

I love this activity because it makes a chore fun. Throw leaves at each other, bury yourself in the leaves, and jump in your pile.

72. Fantasy Shop Date | Inexpensive to Moderate

Visit a lingerie store together. If you are embarrassed to shop local, go to a neighboring city or shop online.

73. Fantasy Sports Draft Date | Free or Inexpensive

Choose a sport you both love and join a fantasy league together. While the draft is the main date, you'll enjoy months of competitive fun as you seek to be the top team in your fantasy league!

74. Farmers Market Date | Inexpensive to Moderate

Stroll through the local farmers market for veggies, fruits, honey, locally grown goods, and seasonal finds.

75. Ferry Ride Date | Inexpensive to Moderate

A ferry is about the cheapest boat tour you can take. Most ferries have cabins to enjoy a bird's eye view, but sometimes we go outside to enjoy the sights and smells of the water.

76. Film a Commercial Date | Free or Inexpensive

Film a product pitch or comedy spoof. Pop popcorn and watch your amusing amateur acting skills!

77. Fireflies Date | Free or Inexpensive
Without harming them, collect fireflies and place them in a clear container. After collecting the fireflies, let them go and enjoy the light show on a blanket and enjoy each other's company.

78. Fireworks Viewing Date | Free or Inexpensive
Fireworks can be viewed at fairs, festivals, and even sporting events.

79. First Impressions Date | Free or Inexpensive
Journal your first impressions, dates, and moments shared during those magical days. Take turns reading your entries and keep these as special documents of your love.

80. FirstAid/CPR Date | Free or Inexpensive
Not very romantic, but taking a first aid and CPR class together will prepare you for an emergency. To lighten the mood, enjoy a meal at a restaurant after the class.

81. Fishing Date | Free or Inexpensive
A relaxing date awaits you. Pack a cooler, snacks, and sunblock. While you may not catch a lot of fish, you'll net some cherished memories.

82. Five Love Languages Date | Free or Inexpensive
The Five Love Languages by Gary Chapman is a great resource for couples. Take the Love Languages quiz and discuss the results over dinner.

83. Flirty First Date | Free or Inexpensive
Schedule to meet your partner somewhere. Introduce yourselves and flirt like you just met. Can you keep a straight face using corny pick up lines?

84. Food Truck Fun Date | Inexpensive to Moderate
Food trucks are everywhere, including at many public events. For added variety, split plates from various vendors.

85. Fort Building Date | Free to Inexpensive

Make a fort with cushions, blankets and crawl into your "cave." There are no rules so go wild! Leave an opening so you can watch a favorite childhood movie together.

86. Front Row Seats Date | Moderate to Pricey

Sit in the front row of a concert as close to center as you can and enjoy a date you'll never forget. To pull this off find smaller venues and be online the second presale tickets go on sale.

87. Fun Dance Date | Inexpensive to Moderate

Many venues offer a beginners lesson before many dances. Put yourself out there, you'll do great!

88. Game Night at Home Date | Free or Inexpensive

Two player games offer an intimate experience. Play multiplayer games for group dates. Refer to chapter 9 for my game recommendations.

89. Gardening Class Date | Free or Inexpensive

If you have interest in gardening, attend local classes for free or very low cost.

90. Genealogy and Family History Date | Free or Inexpensive

Fill in a family tree to learn more about your ancestors. Familysearch.org is a fantastic and free starting point.

91. Geocaching Date | Free or Inexpensive

Geocaching is treasure hunting with a GPS device as your map. Geocaching fanatics have "caches" hidden all over the world. Once you find the geocache, there may be small "treasures" to take.

92. Get Fit Date | Free or Inexpensive

Many couples enjoy working out together. This is a good date to repeat to enjoy greater health and wellbeing.

93. Gift Exchange Date | Inexpensive to Moderate

Purchase or make gifts for each other in three categories: $2 maximum, $10 maximum, and $20 maximum. Agree on at least one gag gift because they can be the most memorable!

94. Gingerbread House Date | Inexpensive to Moderate

Gather the items, turn on some Christmas tunes, and get to work. You can make your own gingerbread houses or make one together. Alternatively, make and decorate cookies.

95. Golf Driving Range Date | Inexpensive to Moderate

I encourage you to film each other's swings. You will laugh as you rewatch your whiffs. Some newer driving ranges are entertainment destinations with refreshments and lounging.

96. Go Karts Race Date | Inexpensive to Moderate

Visit a go kart track and have a race or two. Laughs will surely come as you plop down in the kart and race around the track like the big kids that you are!

97. Grocery Shopping Date | Inexpensive to Moderate

Meander the store aisles to enjoy time with your partner while looking for deals, meal ideas and new products.

98. Hammock Day Dream Date | Free or Inexpensive

On a pretty day, hang your hammocks and enjoy time away from the hustle and bustle. I prefer my own double hammock but you might enjoy a tight snuggle in the same one.

99. Haunted House Date | Inexpensive to Moderate

Cling to each other for comfort in the thrills of a haunted house. Comparable options include haunted trails, hallways, or warehouses.

100. Helicopter Excursion Date | Moderate to Pricey

Take a ride on a helicopter for a bird's eye view of your favorite city or natural attraction. These are often available in tourist destinations. I have done this once, and once was enough for me!

101. Hide and Seek Date | Free or Inexpensive
Relive the thrill of a childhood favorite game. Take turns hiding and seeking each other in your home. This is a very silly date but be willing to be silly.

102. Hike Date | Free or Inexpensive
Hiking dates are economical and a great way to exercise and talk. Bring water, sunblock, and a mini first aid kit.

103. Historic Downtown Date | Inexpensive to Moderate
Stroll through the downtown area of a nearby town. Enjoy visiting new shops and restaurants. Check out the town's events calendar for bonus events.

104. Historic Reenactment Date | Inexpensive to Moderate
Watching an outdoor drama or historical reenactment is a great date for history buffs. Summer and fall months provide the best opportunity for these events.

105. History Museum Date | Free or Inexpensive
Step back in time with a date to a history museum. We love looking at old photos and antiques of days gone by. Most museums are low cost or free!

106. Homemade Ice Cream Churning Date | Free or Inexpensive
Electric and hand churned machines are available. It's important to follow the directions perfectly or you'll end up with a milky slush. Our favorites are vanilla and fresh peach!

107. Horseback Trail Date | Moderate to Pricey | Free or Inexpensive
Make a memorable date on horseback as a couple. Guides are available at many stables. Some venues offer picnic lunches and other romantic offerings.

108. Hot Air Balloon Launch Date | Inexpensive to Moderate
Take in the amazing sight of colorful balloons in the sky. Bring a chair or blanket and enjoy a meal together. If you dare, go aboard one of the balloons for a date in the skies!

109. Ice Skating Date | Inexpensive to Moderate

While malls and indoor rinks are available, many ski resorts have outdoor rinks with incredible backdrops. Don't be afraid to rent a beginners cart!

110. Jigsaw Puzzle Date | Free or Inexpensive

Completing a puzzle is mesmerizing and provides time to connect and talk. We adore Charles Wysocki!

111. Jewelry Crafting Date | Free or Inexpensive

Years ago, we bought material to make bead necklaces. Visit a craft store for everything you need to make earrings, necklaces, or bracelets.

112. Karaoke Date | Free or Inexpensive

Step out of your comfort zone and find a public place to perform. Alternatively, host a karaoke night at home. Rock on!

113. Kayaking Date | Moderate to Pricey

Start in calm waters and work your way to more challenging courses. When in doubt, hire a guide. Always follow safety protocol!

114. Kite Flying Fun Date | Free or Inexpensive

Get a high quality kite and aim for a day with winds in the 5-20 mph range for smooth sailing. Take your love to a new altitude!

115. Kissology Date | Free or Inexpensive

I once came across a series of 1950s postcards of couples kissing. Each card featured a different type of kiss. That gave me the idea to have a date centered around finding and practicing new ways to lock lips.

116. LARPing Date | Inexpensive to Moderate

Live action role playing is the nerdtastic hobby of acting out a fantasy persona with costumes. Craft costumes and accessories and get to roleplaying! Watch *The Sasquatch Gang* for some hilarious LARPing inspiration.

117. Laser Tag Date | Inexpensive to Moderate

Bond together as teammates or spice it up and play on opposite teams! Throw down at the arcade too as most Laser Tag venues have many other amusement options.

118. Last Minute Trip Date | Moderate to Pricy

Be spontaneous by looking for cheap last minute flight or hotel deals and take a quick trip together. One of my favorite trips was accomplished by a rare rush of spontaneity I had.

119. Letter and Postcard Date | Free or Inexpensive

Hand write letters, greeting cards, or postcards to some of your family and friends. They will love receiving mail instead of digital messages.

120. Lighthouse Hunt Date | Free or Inexpensive

Half of the US states have lighthouses, even landlocked Arizona! Some lighthouses are in secluded places so be prepared with provisions to make the trip more enjoyable.

121. Limo Fancy Date | Moderate to Pricey

Arrange for a limo ride to a restaurant or event for an unforgettable date! For an added surprise, have roses or other gifts for your partner in the limo.

122. Line Dance Date | Free or Inexpensive

Line dancing is one of the less awkward dances as you can replicate everyone else. Find a line dancing venue to Cha-Cha or Electric Slide!

123. Love Soundtrack Date | Free or Inexpensive

Each partner contributes their favorite love songs. Once compiled, create a special playlist that is ready to set the mood!

124. Manicure Pedicure Date | Inexpensive to Moderate

This joint grooming date can be rejuvenating. For many of us, the first time can be a bit scary or embarrassing but hopefully the other partner can educate and relax you as you participate.

125. Marathon Date | Free or Inexpensive

Training and participating in a marathon is next level. You'll benefit from each other's encouragement as you train and participate. If only one partner participates, the other partner should attend the marathon for support.

126. Massage at Home Date | Free or Inexpensive

I recommend an adjustable headrest with a face pillow to turn any bed into a massage table. Massage oils, candlelight, and soft music take this date to the next level.

127. Mechanical Bull Riding Date | Inexpensive to Moderate

Here's your chance to be a rodeo stud! My operator started out gentle, but as my confidence rose, so did the intensity of the bull until I flew off. Ride'em cowboy!

128. Meetaversary Date | Inexpensive to Moderate

Plan a special date to celebrate the magical day you first met. Take time to acknowledge your meetaversary!

129. Memory Lane Date | Free or Inexpensive

Spend a night at home watching videos from the past. In addition to home movies, sort through old pictures.

130. Metal Detector Treasure Date | Inexpensive to Moderate

Even if you don't want to purchase a metal detector, rent one and take turns scanning and digging for treasure. This is a popular beach activity but it can be done anywhere.

131. Midnight Eats Date | Inexpensive to Moderate

We have a cool restaurant nearby that stays open all night. Choose a restaurant and enjoy a midnight or very late dinner date.

132. Mini Golf Date | Inexpensive to Moderate

The great American date, mini golf! From the classic orange Putt-Putt to the gimmicky adventure mini golf, they are all a ton of fun.

133. Minute to Win It Date | Free or Inexpensive

It was funny watching Jolene move a cookie from her forehead to her mouth without using her hands. Another favorite is slow dancing with a ping pong ball held in place with only your foreheads!

134. Mission Statement Date | Free to Inexpensive

Develop a mission statement for your family. Find a relaxed restaurant to lounge in as you work out the details. Print the mission statement out to be displayed in your home.

135. Model Construction Date | Inexpensive to Moderate

Get two separate models and spend time together working on your chosen models. There are models for all skill levels from elaborate glue and paint kits to simple snap together varieties.

136. Movie Location Date | Free or Inexpensive

We've enjoyed visiting a few of our favorite movie locations. Take photos in poses from the movie as you enjoy the vibe of the "onset" location.

137. Movie Night at Home Date | Free or Inexpensive

Choose your movie in advance so you don't waste time scrolling for one to watch. Immerse yourself with fresh popcorn, snacks, and your favorite beverage.

138. Movie Roulette Date | Free or Inexpensive

Obtain a list of current movies and randomly choose one to watch together. You can also do this with streaming services if you aren't a fan of theaters.

139. Movies in the Park Date | Free or Inexpensive

Many parks offer free big screen features. Bring snacks, stretch out on a blanket or lawn chair, and enjoy the show. Most cruises also offer outdoor movies on the big screen while at sea.

140. Murder Mystery Date | Inexpensive to Moderate

Many of these are themed and you can dress up in character. Although I am no sleuth, Jolene has solved a few cases!

141. Music Festival Date | Free or Inexpensive

Music festivals are a way to consume large amounts of your favorite music. Festivals usually have plentiful concessions and other local fares to enjoy.

142. Musical Talent Date | Free or Inexpensive

Play instruments or sing with each other. This will be easy if you have musical talent but if not, have patience with each other.

143. Mystical Future Date | Free or Inexpensive

You don't have to be a believer to enjoy this experience. Use tarot cards, fortune cookies, mystical books, and the Magic 8 Ball! I predict a strengthened relationship to those that will embrace silly fun!

144. Magicians Date | Free or Inexpensive

Learn a few magic tricks and present your magic together. For added value, perform it for family and friends. If you get really good, entertain children's groups and adult care centers.

145. My Hometown Date | Inexpensive to Moderate

Show your partner your hometown. Walk through a favorite store, visit the local park, and eat at a restaurant from your childhood. Listen as they tell you about special moments and stories. Do the other hometown next time!

146. Mystery Concert Date | Inexpensive to Moderate

Find a musician you've never heard of and attend their concert. Community concerts and local establishments are great venues to sample new artists.

147. Mystery Location Date | Inexpensive to Moderate

Plan a mystery date for your partner. They will have no idea what activity or restaurant you planned until they arrive. On a future date, swap roles.

148. Mystery Order Restaurant Date | Inexpensive to Moderate

During this dinner date, choose and order each other's meal. This date jostles those who generally order the same thing. Be open-minded!

149. National Park Date | Free or Inexpensive
Spend a day or more visiting a National Park. Check off any parks visited in the National Parks Challenge in Part 3. The quest to visit these parks can become a healthy obsession.

150. Nature Nerds Date | Free or Inexpensive
Identify and learn fun facts about trees, plants, birds, and rocks on a nature walk. In addition to books, online resources are great.

151. Nature Walk Date | Free or Inexpensive
Find a nature walk and stroll together through the wondrous surroundings. Trails with water features can be particularly relaxing.

152. New Hairdo Date | Inexpensive to Moderate
Sample a new hairstyle by getting a fresh cut or use product to shape into a wild new look. This can be serious or silly. Go out sporting the new hairstyle.

153. New Perfume and Cologne Date | Inexpensive to Moderate
Try various perfumes and colognes. Find scents that you both enjoy and purchase a bottle of each. You'll always remember this special date as you apply your chosen fragrance.

154. New Years Resolution and Dinner Date | Inexpensive to Moderate
We traditionally eat collard greens and black-eyed peas on New Year's Day. The greens and peas represent dollars and coins to bring luck to the New Year. Write your personal and couple resolutions and share them with each other.

155. Obstacle Course Date | Inexpensive to Moderate
Exercise with fun competition as you race to the finish line. I loved the *American Gladiators* TV show and this date offers a similar thrill.

156. Odd Festival Date | Inexpensive to Moderate
I found a Blackberry Festival, Livermush Festival, and even a Big Foot Festival all within an hour from my home! Find an odd one near you.

157. Oddball Sports Date | Free or Inexpensive

These sports can include ping-pong, horseshoes, badminton, croquet, bocce, and others. Community centers, campgrounds, and resorts often offer them at no cost.

158. Olympics Day Date | Free or Inexpensive

Compete against yourself and your partner in Olympic-themed events. You can revisit this event on future dates and try to beat your previous Olympic records!

159. Orchard or Berry Patch Date | Inexpensive to Moderate

Pick your favorite fruits or berries together! Many orchards are branching out to include new products, activities, and additional ways to enjoy your visit.

160. Ornament Creation Date | Free or Inexpensive

Make ornaments together. We've used Scrabble tiles to make name ornaments. Play Christmas music or a movie in the background.

161. Paddle Boat Date | Inexpensive to Moderate

Every couple needs to try this once! Because paddle boats are often found in parks, take a picnic with you!

162. Paintball or Airsoft Date | Inexpensive to Moderate

Play as a team or work against each other for bragging rights. This is a great group date but follow all safety instructions and be prepared for a small sting.

163. Paper and Origami Date | Free or Inexpensive

We've had some great paper airplane competitions from our elevated back deck. Make fun creations from paper. Invest in a variety of high quality origami paper to dive in!

164. Park and Make-Out Date | Free or Inexpensive

Relive the teenage dream at a sizzling spot. While traditionally done in a car, you could also find a secluded spot in a park or on a hike. Don't forget breath mints!

165. Passport Date | Inexpensive to Moderate

Complete the requirements to obtain passports together. After obtaining the passport, plot an international trip together!

166. Perfume and Cologne Date | Inexpensive to Moderate

Join each other for a visit to your favorite cosmetics shop and sample different scents. Find one that you both love and make a purchase if you find your perfect scent.

167. Petting Zoo Date | Inexpensive to Moderate

The big kid comes out at a petting zoo as animals surround you in hopes of getting petted. Rescued animals seem to have a heightened appreciation for being loved on, so love away.

168. Photo Shoot Date | Free or Inexpensive

Photo shoots are a fun way to appreciate each other and capture your love on film. Shopping for clothes and props can be as fun as the photo shoot itself. I particularly enjoyed a couples photoshoot based on the silly engagement photos in Jared Hess' *Masterminds*.

169. Pickleball Date | Free or Inexpensive

Pickleball is growing at an incredible pace because it's easy to learn for a wide range of people. If you've ever played tennis, you'll pick this up in no time. This has become one of my favorite sports to play.

170. Picnic at a Park Date | Inexpensive to Moderate

The quintessential date that many of us have never done. Pack your basket, relax on a cute blanket, and enjoy serenity together.

171. Pizzeria at Home Date | Free to Inexpensive

Gather all of your favorite ingredients and make homemade pizza together. I love pre-made thin crusts. Play Italian music for extra flair. I love using my Super Mario voice as I boisterously make my pizza.

172. Play Dress Up Date | Free or Inexpensive
A party or holiday with a theme is a good time to visit the dress up bin and have fun. Some community events encourage costumes.

173. Playground Pals Date | Free or Inexpensive
Revisit the silly games of your childhood. Swing together or just relax. Pick a time when it's not crowded. We don't need children getting trampled by lovers in the park!

174. Playing in the Rain Date | Free or Inexpensive
Lay on the ground or porch and let the rain fall. The second half of this date could be a hot shower and a warm snuggle under the covers!

175. Poetry Date | Free or Inexpensive
I love using words to share my feelings. Write each other a poem. This can be rudimentary or something more lengthy. Consider writing a sentimental one and a silly one. Share your poetry with each other over a romantic dinner out.

176. Pottery Date | Inexpensive to Moderate
Attend a pottery class for sculpting fun. As a bonus, you'll have a piece of pottery to commemorate your date adventure.

177. Progressive Dinner Date | Inexpensive to Moderate
Have an appetizer at one restaurant, your entree at the next, and dessert at the last. Mix and match your favorite spots for an unforgettable meal.

178. Public Transportation Date | Inexpensive to Moderate
We sometimes use public transportation for the entirety of our trips. The adventure of riding and seeing the many stops is so much fun. When visiting a city, use transportation as a mini date as you go to your destinations.

179. Pumpkin Carving Date | Free or Inexpensive
Have a fun competition with a spooky, funny, or serious theme. If you are competitive, send photos for your family and friends to pick the best pumpkin. Bake the pumpkin seeds if you enjoy eating them!

180. Pumpkin Patch Date | Inexpensive to Moderate
Pumpkin patches have evolved into an autumnal experience with more than just pumpkins. Usually they have seasonal refreshments, hay rides, games, playgrounds, and petting farms!

181. Quilt Square Trail Drive Date | Free or Inexpensive
Communities of people display them on their barns and houses. Visit a quilt square trail. Enjoy sightseeing as you hunt for these roadside designs!

182. RC Cars, Planes, or Boats Date | Inexpensive to Moderate
There are many RC vehicle options with some being much more friendly for beginners than others. Alternatively, fly a drone.

183. Record Player Retro Date | Free or Inexpensive
Record players have made an inconceivable return. Purchase a record player and go on a date to find some records you want to listen to together. Enjoy the night as you listen to your favorite records.

184. Re-enact Vintage Photos Date | Free or Inexpensive
Re-enact treasured vintage photos like a "before and after." If you're a young couple, hold on to the clothes in your favorite couples photos. Doing this will be that much better in the future!

185. Renaissance Festivals Date | Inexpensive to Moderate
Traveling medieval shows are a fun time machine! Watch knights jousts, magicians dazzle, and hypnotists entertain!

186. Retro Arcade Date | Inexpensive to Moderate
Classic arcades are making a comeback. The sights and sounds of the games are incredibly nostalgic. Many have a flat fee for the entire day.

187. River Boat Cruise Date | Moderate to Pricey
Take a dinner or river cruise! Bigger boats often offer meals or dancing. We enjoyed a Mark Twain themed cruise on the Mississippi. We went on a week day and there were only a handful of people with us. Roam the boat and go up top for amazing views!

188. River Rafting Date | Moderate to Pricey

Book a guide and hit the rapids! This exhilarating date will surely be a memorable experience. Stay within your ability level while doing this thrilling date as being thrown out of the raft isn't very fun.

189. River Tubing Date | Inexpensive to Moderate

We giggled, wiggled, and splashed our way down the Chattahoochee River. Tubing is an economical way to spend a day on the water and generally safer than the above mentioned river rafting.

190. Roadside Attraction Date | Free or Inexpensive

From the world's largest easel in Kansas to the world's largest chest of drawers in North Carolina. Start your own journey of finding these unique roadside attractions.

191. Rodeo Date | Inexpensive to Moderate

Dress up like cowboys and enjoy the rodeo. In addition to roaming rodeos there are stationary rodeo themed venues that could be visited as well. We have visited several in Oklahoma and Texas. Yeehaw!

192. Rock, Gem, and Gold Date | Free or Inexpensive

Explore a creek and admire the rocks and minerals. For a manufactured experience, visit a "gem mine" that stocks material for guaranteed finds.

193. Rock Art Date | Free or Inexpensive

Paint anything you want on your small smooth river rocks. I like to use a clear sealant when the paint dries.

194. Roller Skating Date | Inexpensive to Moderate

Enjoy the retro sights, sounds, and smells of the roller rink! Unlike those awkward teenage years, you're guaranteed a couples' skate!

195. Romantic Fireplace Date | Free or Inexpensive

Is there anything more romantic than snuggling in the wispy flicker of a fireplace? Don't fret if you don't have a fireplace. Stream one on a device or rent a place with a fireplace.

196. Ropes Course Date | Inexpensive to Moderate
The feeling of accomplishment after completing the course will be a fantastic memory together. These courses can be found in amusement parks, wilderness areas, and even on the deck of cruise ships!

197. Run/Walk/Jog a 5K Date | Free or Inexpensive
Encourage each other as you work your way to the finish line. You do not need to be a seasoned track star to complete a 5K. Many people gently jog or even walk. This empowering date can bring you close together and improve your health.

198. Sand Castle Date | Free or Inexpensive
Work together to create a masterpiece in the sand. A bucket and shovel is all you need for a great day at the beach. Don't limit yourself to just sand castles, let your artistic talent shine.

199. Sand Dunes Date | Free or Inexpensive
Spend a day playing in nature's sandbox. I loved throwing Frisbee and running in the sand dunes to catch it.

200. Scavenger Hunt Date | Free or Inexpensive
Make a themed scavenger hunt or use a previously designed one. There are also community scavenger hunts, often featuring prizes.

201. Science Experiment Date | Free or Inexpensive
Revisit your school science experiments as a couple! Try the Mentos and Coke experiment and the classic volcano with baking soda and vinegar!

202. Science Museum Date | Inexpensive to Moderate
Explore fossils, planetary wonders, 4D theaters, and other unique displays at a science museum. One of my favorite dates is when in new cities with large museums.

203. Seashell and Seaglass Hunt Date | Free or Inexpensive
Stroll the beach for that perfect shell, seaglass, or other rare find. For bonus Mother Earth points, bag up old fishing line and other trash.

204. Second Chance Prom Date | Inexpensive to Moderate
Attend a second chance prom with your partner. If you can't find a second chance prom, attend a formal dance or event and treat it like a prom.

205. Second First Date Date | Free or Inexpensive
A reenactment of your first date can be both nostalgic and exciting. Retrace your steps as you replay the date.

206. Self-Defense Class Date | Inexpensive to Moderate
This date will bring you together as you become more prepared for uncertainty. Not only is this date good for learning self defense but also for exercise.

207. Sensory Date | Free or Inexpensive
The receiving partner is blindfolded while the giver gently rubs, massages, and tickles the receiver's skin with the items. Switch roles. Items can include feathers, back scratchers, leather, and even a piece of ice.

208. Sign Language Date | Free or Inexpensive
Learn a few basic signs. The alphabet should be your first goal because you can spell out anything once you learn all the letters. Suggested words to learn are: I love you, ready to go, bathroom, food, and drink.

209. Skiing or Tubing Date | Moderate to Pricey
A ski resort or tubing facility provides a picturesque and fun date. Be prepared with appropriate clothing so you can fully enjoy this chilly date.

210. Skydiving Date | Moderate to Pricey
Plan it together as you wouldn't want to surprise your partner with this. For a lower thrill, consider indoor skydiving.

211. Sleep on the Beach Date | Free or Inexpensive
On your next beach trip, take a blanket and spend the night nestled together on the beach. You don't need to stay the whole night.

212. Snorkeling or Scuba Date | Moderate to Pricey

Snorkeling is a simple way to bond while enjoying a unique view of the underwater world. Scuba diving is next level for the more adventurous couple.

213. Snowman Date | Free to Inexpensive

Relive the joy of youth with a snow outing. Make snow angels, build a fort, create a snowman, go sledding, or even have a snowball fight. If you don't live in an area that gets snow, take a trip somewhere that does.

214. Snow Much Fun Date | Free or Inexpensive

Relive the joy of youth with a snow outing. Make snow angels, build a fort, create a snowman, go sledding, or even have a snowball fight. If you don't live in an area that gets snow, take a trip somewhere that does.

215. Solar Eclipse Date | Free or Inexpensive

You will remember this bucket list phenomenon forever. I loved how it fooled the frogs and grasshoppers into making their evening noises.

216. Space View Date | Free or Inexpensive

Astronomy clubs and universities occasionally open to the public. If you can't access an observatory, try a planetarium or even skywatching on a clear, dark night.

217. Special Event Date | Inexpensive to Moderate

This date takes you to an event that is special to you. I attended a *Gilligan's Island* event at a local theater with a crowd of other classic TV fanatics. This is an ideal way to love on your partner by taking them to a special event they enjoy, even if it's not your favorite. Remember, if something is important to your partner, make it important to you!

218. Speedway Date | Inexpensive to Moderate

I'm not into racing but I loved a "Tour of Destruction" event with a demolition derby, monster trucks, and even a jet engine that melted a car!

219. Sporting Event Date | Inexpensive to Moderate
Choose a sporting event to attend together. If you have a favorite team dress up and make a fun date out of the team as you cheer them to victory.

220. Spring Clean Date | Free or Inexpensive
Schedule a time and work together to tackle a few spring cleaning tasks. To make the mundane more magical, turn up your favorite music and dance as you clean.

221. Stand Up Comedy Date | Inexpensive to Moderate
Spend a date working on your own stand up comedy routine. If you feel confident, participate in an open mic night. If you are too shy for the spotlight, perform for friends and family. Alternatively, watch a live comedian.

222. Stargazing Date | Free or Inexpensive
There are books and apps to help you identify planets and constellations. I stargazed in a Nevada desert and seeing the vibrant Milky Way Galaxy was one of the most breathtaking moments of my life.

223. State Park Date | Inexpensive to Moderate
Visit a state park. Select one you have never been to or revisit a favorite. Adventure tip: Get a map or take a photo of any maps and park information before exploring so you get full value from the experience!

224. Stay in Bed Date | Free or Inexpensive
Relax, sleep, talk, fall back asleep. This date can slow down your mind and help you bond in the warmth of your sheets.

225. Sunday Afternoon Drive Date | Free or Inexpensive
It doesn't matter where you go, it's about relaxed quality time with each other while seeing new things.

226. Sunrise or Sunset Date | Free or Inexpensive
Find a place where you can see a sunrise or sunset. Beaches and mountains are wonderful places for this date.

227. Surf, Skim, Body Board Date | Inexpensive to Moderate

On your next beach trip, try any of the above activities together. A simple raft or boogie board is also an excellent option to ride waves. You can hire a guide, as needed.

228. Symphony or Orchestra Date | Inexpensive to Moderate

From classic masterpieces to modern music, a symphony or orchestra can be a classy twist on the standard concert.

229. Tacky Thrift Store Date | Inexpensive to Moderate

Search thrift stores for the tackiest, ugliest, or funniest clothing items. The fun continues during a date night in the tacky clothing to miniature golf, bowling or other location!

230. Tandem Bike Ride Date | Inexpensive to Moderate

While a tandem bike is a lot to own and transport, you can rent them at many places with trails, river walks, and boardwalks.

231. Taste Test Date | Free or Inexpensive

Conduct a blind taste test with multiple brands of the same items to decide which is really the best. We gathered a few chicken sandwiches from different restaurants and were able to declare our ultimate "winner."

232. Technology Free Date | Free or Inexpensive

Leave all your electronic devices at home, including your phone, and take a date night of your choice. After the initial panic of not having electronics, settle into each other's undivided attention.

233. Tennis Date | Free or Inexpensive

This can be a simple volley or a serious match as long as you're having fun. An ideal date to invite another couple so you can play both together and against each other.

234. Tent Camping Date | Free or Inexpensive

Wilderness areas, campgrounds, and even your own backyard can be a spot to camp. I have included a camping checklist in Part 3 for your consideration.

235. Theater, Drama, or Play Date | Inexpensive to Moderate

Add a little culture to the relationship by attending a live show. I favor comedies and loved the *Clue* play but I also enjoy every version of *A Christmas Carol*.

236. Time Capsule Date | Inexpensive to Moderate

Create a small time capsule to be opened in the future. Each partner writes a letter to their future selves. Add fun things such as clothes, catalogs, and trinkets.

237. Tourist Trap Date | Inexpensive to Moderate

We have a few "tourist traps" nearby that I have avoided most of my life. One day we decided to try The Blowing Rock and I loved it. Try one near you!

238. Train Ride Date | Moderate to Pricey

Choose a destination and arrive by train! There are brief and extended train excursions and some even offer dinner! We loved Tweetsie Railroad which is a very short wild west themed ride.

239. Trampoline Park Date | Inexpensive to Moderate

Most parks offer multiple activities such as jousting, foam pits, and warped walls. I suggest offtimes or right when it opens so the venue has fewer people to navigate around.

240. Trivia Night Date | Free or Inexpensive

Test your combined brain power as you compete in trivia. Many restaurants and venues host trivia nights but these can be hosted at your home too. This is a great double or triple date.

241. Try a New Restaurant Date | Inexpensive to Moderate

Break free of going to the same places and occasionally try restaurants you've never been to. You might hit a dud, but you might find a new favorite!

242. Ultimate Guide Date | Free or Inexpensive

Spend a date completing the Ultimate Guide for your partner. Use this priceless information to love on your partner purposefully and intentionally.

243. Valentine's Day Date | Inexpensive to Moderate

A romantic dinner for two is an ideal date. A very attentive partner can set this date up with a cute invitation and roses.

244. Vacation Planning Date | Free or Inexpensive

I love exploring maps for new travel destinations and researching activities and adventures. Work out fun itineraries for your proposed destinations.

245. Video Game Date | Free or Inexpensive

There are many cooperative and non-traditional video game options. Party and mini games are highly recommended.

246. Volunteer your Talent Date | Free or Inexpensive

Jolene has volunteered her sign language talents at schools, churches, and senior groups and it melts my heart. Whatever your talents, volunteer them together.

247. Water Fun at Home Date | Free or Inexpensive

Enjoy the outdoors with water sprinklers, water balloons, or homemade water slides to relive the golden childhood summers.

248. Water Park Fun Date | Moderate to Pricey

Fun-filled shrieks and uncontrollable laughter down a water slide are unforgettable. If you aren't feeling daring, enjoy a relaxing lazy river.

249. Waterfall Hikes Date | Free or Inexpensive

Few hikes pay off like ones with a majestic, peaceful waterfall. Pack a swimsuit and towel, just in case!

250. Wild West Date | Inexpensive to Moderate

Visit an old west themed park or event. We attended a Wild West reenactment in Wichita, Kansas at "Old Cow Town," witnessing a gunfight between the Marshall and some naughty bandits.

251. Winter Hike Date | Free or Inexpensive

If you aren't a fan of crowds or heat, you'll enjoy a winter hike. Walking the wilderness in the winter has its own magical aura…and almost no poesky insects.

252. Wreath Creating Date | Inexpensive to Moderate

Jolene once crafted a beautiful seasonal wreath and I accidentally donated it to a local thrift store. To make amends, I went with her to purchase new wreath materials which became the inspiration for this date!

253. Wrestling Date | Inexpensive to Moderate

Wrestlers put a lot of work into the craft and put on an amazing show. I prefer local wrestling events that are affordable but larger scale events are an option.

254. Yoga/Mindfulness Date | Free or Inexpensive

Yoga and mindfulness calms us from our hectic lifestyles. Enjoy the calming stillness and purposeful movements.

255. Zip Lining Date | Moderate to Pricey

Ziplining can be an adrenaline rush for couples who thrive on high adventure. As a bonus, most zip lines are in beautiful locations for hiking and other activities.

256. Zoo Date | Inexpensive to Moderate

Walk around a zoo on a date and you might be surprised at your childlike wonder. Some zoos serve as rehabilitation centers for wounded animals so your attendance supports a good cause.

The Relationship Roadmap Dating Adventure Score and Title

To motivate you to go on more dates, I've devised a rating scale that ranks your dating adventure level. Tally all the dates you've completed from the list above to claim your official dating adventure score and title! I hope you'll increase your score and more importantly nurture your relationship in adventurous ways!

Total number of dates: _____   Today's Date: _____

Updated number of dates: _____   Today's Date: _____

Updated number of dates: _____   Today's Date: _____

Updated number of dates: _____   Today's Date: _____

Updated number of dates: _____   Today's Date: _____

Updated number of dates: _____   Today's Date: _____

Bronze

0 = You must've met 10 minutes ago

1-9 = New Acquaintances

10-19 = Getting Familiar

20-29 = Friendly Visitors

30-39 = Loyal Loungers

40-49 = Jolly Journeyers

Silver

50-59 = Bosom Buddies

60-69 = Fun Followers

70-79 = Playful Duo

80-89 = Adorable Amigos

90-99 = Hobnobbing Heartthrobs

Gold

100-109 = Sightseeing Seers

110-119 = Acolytes of Adventure

120-129 = Divine Everlasting Tourists

130-139 = Celebrated Vacationologists

140-149 = Pulchritudinous Passport Pilgrims

Platinum

150-159 = Almighty Thrilling Crusaders

160-169 = Audacious Adventuring Pals

170-179 = Jovial Pioneering Twosome

180-189 = Celebrators of Togetherness

190-199 = Vivacious Socialite Vacationeers

Diamond

200-209 = Illustrious Global Explorers

210-219 = Everlasting Kingly Gazetteers

220-229 = Exclusive Angelic Partners

230-239 = Adventure Quest Companions

240-249 = Exotic Voyaging Excursionists

God Tier

250+= Immortal and Ethereal Eternal Realm of Elite Dating Celestial Deity

At the time of writing this, I'm a level 158 Platinum Almighty Thrilling Crusader! What level are you? Boost your score over the coming days, months, and years!

Part 5
Relationship Extras, Challenges, Mantras, Surveys, and Checklists

The Relationship Roadmap 100+ Terms of Endearment

We all have cute and fun nicknames and terms of endearment that we use with our lovers. For fun, I've compiled a list to help you add some flair to the notes you write, texts you send, or even your everyday conversations. These terms span multiple decades, so feel free to mix in some vintage endearments.

Adorable	Doll	Hot Stuff	Precious
Angel	Doll Face	Hun	Precious Angel
Angelic Face	Doughnut Hole	Hunk	Prince Charming
Angelic Body	Dream Boat	Hunny	Princess
Babe	Dream Girl	Hunny Buns	Pucker Puss
Baby	Dream Guy	Juicy	Pudding
Baby Boy	Dreamy	Kinky Winky	Punkin'
Baby Cakes	Dumpling	Kitten	Queen
Baby Doll	Dynamite	Knockout	Rock Star
Baby Dumpling	Eternal Love	Love	Sassy
Baby Girl	Ecstasy	Love Bug	Sex Pot
Bae	Fire	Love of my Life	Sexy
Beautiful	Firecracker	Luscious	Shuggey
Beefcake	Flame	Luscious Lips	Sizzle
Beloved	Fruit Lips	Love Muffin	Skank Biscuit
Better Half	Goddess	Lovey	Slice of Pie
Boo	Gorgeous	Monkey Butt	Snuggle Bear
Boopie	Gummy Bear	Muffin	Soulmate
Bunny	Gum Drop	My Rock	Spunky
Buttercup	Handsome	My Main Squeeze	Stud
Chunky Monkey	Hard Body	My Man	Sugar Bear
Cinnamon Lips	Hearts Desire	My Fave	Super Man
Cuddle Cake	Hercules	One and Only	Super Woman
Cupcake	Hey Girl	Other Half	Sweetie
Cutie	Honey	Peach Pie	Sweetheart
Cutie Pie	Hot	Peanut	Sweetness
Darling	Hot Lips	Pet	Sweet Thang
Dazzler	Hotness	Perfection	Teddy Bear
Dear	Hottest	Pin Up Model	Tiger
Dearest	Hot Pants	Pookie	Wonderful
	Hotty Potaty		

The Relationship Roadmap 18 Flirtatious Flaunts

These flirty activities offer romantic ways to express your love for your partner. Try a few and see if your relationship heats up!

1. Winking—a flirtatious gesture that can signal desire and spark excitement.
2. Try on sexy clothes and send flirty selfies from the store dressing room.
3. Record your love story or memories then share them with your partner.
4. Use a clothing item from your partner's wardrobe, snap photos while wearing it.
5. Wear your partner's hoodie and let them know it makes you feel closer to them.
6. Turn down the sheets and create a lovely, effortless entrance into bed.
7. Learn the American Sign Language sign for "I Love You" and use it as a sweet gesture.
8. Leave love notes hidden around the house for your partner to discover.
9. Gently massage your partner's feet for a refreshing treat, just because.
10. Write a short poem expressing your love for your partner.
11. Slip sexy undergarments into their briefcase, purse, or daypack for a surprising find!
12. Have roses delivered to your partner as a romantic surprise.
13. Write their name and a heart in the sand at the beach—let them find it.
14. Surprise your partner by mailing them a greeting card.
15. Include love notes or sweet sentiments with any gift or gesture as desired.
16. Get real or artificial mistletoe, hold it over your partner, and enjoy a playful kiss.
17. Surprise your partner with an invitation to meet at home for lunch or a romantic rendezvous.
18. Take their lunch order, deliver it to their workplace, and, if possible, enjoy lunch together.

The Relationship Roadmap Couple Merit Badges

As an Eagle Scout, I loved earning merit badges. In scouting, achieving a certain level of knowledge or skill in a subject earns you a patch that signifies your competence. Reflecting on the gaps in our experiences, I was inspired by the thrill of collecting those badges. Now, you and your partner can "earn" your own couple merit badges! These badges set goals to try new activities together and keep the excitement alive in your relationship. See if you can earn them all!

Merit Badge Checklist

☐ Art Appreciation Badge   ☐ Money Management Badge

☐ Camping Together Badge   ☐ Movie Night Badge

☐ Cooking Together Badge   ☐ Photography Badge

☐ Dancing Together Badge   ☐ Picnic Together Badge

☐ Emergency Planning Badge   ☐ Restaurant Variety Badge

☐ Gaming Together Badge   ☐ Social Butterfly Badge

☐ Gardening Together Badge   ☐ Water Adventure Badge

☐ Home Improvement Badge   ☐ Wilderness Exploration Badge

Badge Requirements

☐ **Art Appreciation Badge**

    ☐ Visit an art museum or gallery, share your favorite pieces, and explain why you like them.

    ☐ Create a piece of art for each other.

☐ **Camping Together Badge**

    ☐ Plan an overnight trip together.

    ☐ Tent or RV camp together.

☐ **Cooking Together Badge**

    ☐ Plan and prepare a meal together.

    ☐ Try a new food that neither of you has tasted before.

☐ **Dancing Together Badge**

    ☐ Dance as a couple at home to music.

    ☐ Dance as a couple at a public event.

☐ **Emergency Planning Badge**

    ☐ Create an emergency kit for each vehicle.

    ☐ Create an emergency kit for your home.

☐ **Gaming Together Badge**

    ☐ Revisit and play a classic favorite game.

    ☐ Pick out and play a new game together.

☐ **Gardening Together Badge**

    ☐ Plant a flower or vegetable together.

    ☐ Harvest and enjoy a flower or vegetable together.

☐ **Home Improvement Badge**

    ☐ Create a list of projects you'd each like to complete.

    ☐ Choose one project and complete it together.

☐ **Money Management Badge**

    ☐ Calculate your exact amount of debt.

    ☐ Calculate your total assets (home, auto, savings, retirement, etc.).

    ☐ Consider ways to strengthen your current financial situation.

☐ **Movie Night Badge**

    ☐ Choose your favorite movie that your partner hasn't seen and watch it together.

    ☐ Go to a theater and watch a movie together.

☐ **Photography Badge**

    ☐ Sort through photos together, pick your all-time favorite photo of your partner alone and as a couple, share them, and explain why you love them.

    ☐ Take a few new silly, serious, and cute photos together.

☐ **Picnic Together Badge**

    ☐ Choose a spot and plan a picnic together.

    ☐ Go on a picnic.

☐ **Restaurant Variety Badge**

    ☐ Try a new dish at your favorite restaurant.

    ☐ Visit a new restaurant neither of you has tried.

☐ **Social Butterfly Badge**

    ☐ Invite a new couple for a double date.

    ☐ Attend a new social event together.

☐ **Water Adventure Badge**

    ☐ Swim together at a pool or swim spot.

    ☐ Go tubing, paddling, or rafting together.

☐ **Wilderness Exploration Badge**

    ☐ Visit a local park neither of you has been to.

    ☐ Visit a state or national park neither of you has explored.

The Relationship Roadmap Couple Merit Badges Rank!

1–5 Badges: Beginning Beavers Scout Couple

6–10 Badges: Cheerful Chipmunks Scout Couple

11–14 Badges: Foxy Foxes Scout Couple

All 15 Badges: Flying Eagles Scout Couple

The Relationship Roadmap Ultimate Guide to:

_____

Important Dates:
- Birthday: _____
- Meetaversary: _____
- Anniversary: _____

My Partner's Sizes:
- Pant: _____
- Shirt: _____
- Ring _____
- Other: _____

My Partner's Favorite Things:
-
-
-

My Partner's Favorite Restaurants, Food, and Snacks:
-
-
-

Gift Ideas for my Partner:
-
-

Places My Partner Wants to Travel:
-
-

My Partner's Favorite Music Artists (Concert Ideas):
-
-

My Partner's Love Languages:
-
-

The Relationship Roadmap Ultimate Guide to:

Important Dates:
- Birthday: _____
- Meetaversary: _____
- Anniversary: _____

My Partner's Sizes:
- Pant: _____
- Ring _____
- Shirt: _____
- Other: _____

My Partner's Favorite Things:
-
-
-

My Partner's Favorite Restaurants, Food, and Snacks:
-
-
-

Gift Ideas for my Partner:
-
-

Places My Partner Wants to Travel:
-
-

My Partner's Favorite Music Artists (Concert Ideas):
-
-

My Partner's Love Languages:
-
-

The Relationship Roadmap Mantra Compilation

I summarized the end of each chapter with a mantra or self-talk statement. What you tell yourself impacts your emotions. Be sure you tell yourself uplifting and inspiring things every day. These positive affirmations are meant to be read and reread.

Mantra #1 | Our Importance to Each Other

We have a rich history together. Of all the people we could be with, we chose each other. My partner is an important part of my world.

Mantra #2 | Our Past and Our Future

We come from different backgrounds with unique experiences. The individual choices we made led us to each other. Together we will create a beautiful path into the future.

Mantra #3 | Communication

I will be transparent with my partner while building a foundation of trust and support. I will improve communication and assure that we understand each other. I'll offer ample grace as we work toward a mutually gratifying relationship.

Mantra #4 | Problem Solving

While life can be hard, I will find success for myself and my relationship. We will overcome setbacks and find beautifully smooth solutions.

Mantra #5 | Goals

I have goals that I will accomplish. As I pursue my own goals I will also encourage my partner in their goals. Together we will overcome all setbacks. We will accomplish our unified goals.

Mantra #6 | Family Life

We will work together for the betterment of our family. We will find balance through unsettling times. As challenges with children or other family members arise we will encompass all with love and security.

Mantra #7 | Appearance and Grooming

Caring for myself will allow me to take greater pride in my appearance. I don't need to compare my looks to anyone else, I am uniquely special and I will become the best me!

Mantra #8 | Accepting Change

As I expand my comfort zone I will become more flexible to new adventures. I will accept and embrace change. I will thrive!

Mantra #9 | Activities Together and Apart

Life will be enjoyed more fully as I engage in hobbies and activities. While I can share these events with my partner, I will also enjoy time on my own. Traditions will be cherished yet flexible.

Mantra #10 | Through Sickness and Health

Trials and tribulations will come but I will confidently continue my journey through life. When health or other concerns arise, so will I. I will endure all obstacles.

Mantra #11 | Comparisons and Appreciation

In a world of comparisons I will confidently and proudly be myself. My self worth will not be measured by others' success or failure. I am incredibly special and unique.

Mantra #12 | Humor

Laughter and humor lighten my day and gladden my heart. I have the ability to laugh at myself and enjoy the laughter and humor of others.

Mantra #13 | Finances

I can govern my spending while investing in my future. I am optimistic about my economic security and the achievement of financial freedom.

Mantra #14 | Sexual Connection

I will cherish and honor my partner. Intimacy is a gift I'll care for and nurture as I grow my capacity to give and accept mutually gratifying sexual connection.

Mantra #15 | Unique Love Needs

We are all unique in the way we want to be loved. I'll clearly express my desires and seek to understand and meet the needs of my partner.

Mantra #16 | Gifts

The gifts I offer will be well planned and thoughtfully given. I'll accept gifts with gratitude and appreciation.

Mantra #17 | Documenting Life

Our history is special. I can preserve memories with journals, words, photos, and keepsakes. Our legacy will gladden my heart and satisfy my spirit.

Mantra #18 | Perfectly Imperfect

My relationship may not be perfect but it will be strengthened with grace. I will live my best life and enhance my relationship forward, togetherful.

Bonus Mantra | Adventure and Excitement

My present is a blank canvas and I will paint it with new and fulfilling activities. Embracing adventure will keep life fresh and exciting.

The Relationship Roadmap Couples Mini Journal

Reminisce together and make lists and journal entries for the following topics…

Concerts Attended Together
-
-

Movies/TV We Both Adore
-
-

Coolest Gifts To Each Other
-
-

Funniest Moments
-
-

Favorite Vacations
-
-

Places Lived
-
-

Favorite Restaurants/Meals
-
-

Shared Traditions
-
-

Games We Both Love
-
-

Dating Profile and Conversation Starters
Partner #1 _____

Age: _____

Height: _____

Zodiac Sign: _____

Three words to describe me: _____, _____, _____

Qualities I am looking for in a partner: _____

My favorite hobbies: _____, _____, _____

My ideal weekend: _____

_____

My favorite holiday: _____

Morning or night?: _____

Beach or mountains?: _____

I would most want to live in this fictional world: _____

My role models: _____, _____, _____

My phobias/fears: _____, _____, _____

The best day of my life: _____

_____

The best gifts I received as a...

    Child: _____, _____, _____

    Adult: _____, _____, _____

The scariest thing I have ever done: _____

My favorite Halloween costume I wore as a...

    Child: _____, _____, _____

    Adult: _____, _____, _____

My proudest accomplishments: _____, _____

My favorite childhood movies and TV shows:

_____, _____, _____

The person who would play me in a movie: _____

The most famous people I've met: _____, _____

My love languages: _____, _____

Dating Profile and Conversation Starters
Partner #2 _____

Age: _____

Height: _____

Zodiac Sign: _____

Three words to describe me: _____, _____, _____

Qualities I am looking for in a partner: _____, _____

My favorite hobbies: _____, _____, _____

My ideal weekend: _____
_____

My favorite holiday: _____

Morning or night?: _____

Beach or mountains?: _____

I would most want to live in this fictional world: _____

My role models: _____, _____, _____

My phobias/fears: _____, _____, _____

The best day of my life: _____
_____

The best gifts I received as a...

    Child: _____, _____, _____

    Adult: _____, _____, _____

The scariest thing I have ever done: _____

My favorite Halloween costume I wore as a...

    Child: _____, _____, _____

    Adult: _____, _____, _____

My proudest accomplishments: _____, _____

My favorite childhood movies and TV shows:
_____, _____, _____

The person who would play me in a movie: _____

The most famous people I've met: _____, _____

My love languages: _____, _____

The Relationship Roadmap Family Medicine Cabinet Checklist

Here is a list of items that we keep on hand. Adjust to meet your needs. Secure and childproof containers as needed.

Aches & Pains
- Acetaminophen
- Ibuprofen
- Aspirin

Flu, Cold, & Cough
- Decongestants
- Cough Syrup
- Cough Drops
- Menthol Ointment
- Thermometer

Stomach & Digestion
- Antacids
- Anti-diarrheal
- Constipation Relief
- Activated Charcoal

Eye Care
- Eye Drops
- Contacts & Solution

Books
- (Suggested Below)

Baby Specific
- Infant Fever & Pain Medication
- Baby Thermometer
- Diaper Rash Ointment
- Teething Gel
- Suction Bulb

Allergy Medication
- Diphenhydramine
- Loratadine
- OTC Allergy

Skin & Wound
- Bandages
- Sterile Gauze Pads & Rolls
- Adhesive Tape
- Triple Antibiotic Ointment
- Hydrocortisone Cream
- Anti-fungal Ointment
- Calamine Lotion
- Aloe Vera Gel
- Sunscreen

Miscellaneous
- Lip Balm
- Motion Sickness Medication
- Muscle Pain Cream
- Hemorrhoidal Supplies
- Petroleum Jelly
- Tissues
- Cotton Balls & Swabs
- Alcohol
- Hydrogen Peroxide
- Vitamins & Supplements
- Wet Wipes

Hard Core Additions
- Stethoscope
- Blood Pressure Cuff
- Medical Devices
- Nail Clippers
- Tweezers
- Medical Gloves
- Heating Pad
- Ice Packs

Emergency Preparedness and Emergency Medical Books:

- *Are You Ready? An In-Depth Guide to Citizen Preparedness* FEMA Ready
- *The Survival Medicine Handbook* by Joseph and Amy Alton
- *When All Hell Breaks Loose* by Cody Lundin
- *The Encyclopedia of Country Living* by Carla Emery
- *Store This, Not That!* by Crystal Godfrey and Debbie Kent

The Relationship Roadmap Preparedness Plan and Checklist

Jolene, a former FEMA worker, saw firsthand the challenges faced by those affected by disasters. She observed the logistical difficulties in securing and distributing relief amidst threats like hurricanes, tornadoes, floods, wildfires, and power outages.

Couples and families should maintain a preparedness plan and supplies for two key reasons. First, help may not arrive immediately after a disaster, leaving you to fend for yourself. Second, having your own supplies reduces pressure on limited resources, allowing responders to prioritize those in greatest need.

The Basics (Short-Term Preparedness):

- 3+ day supply of water
- 3+ day supply of non-perishable food and a manual can opener
- Medical kit and medications (see family medicine cabinet checklist)
- Tent and sleeping bag (for evacuation)
- Flashlights and extra batteries
- Battery- or crank-powered radio
- Thick plastic sheeting, paracord rope, and high-quality duct tape
- Basic tools
- Backpacks or 5-gallon buckets (for evacuation)
- Positive attitude, humor, and optimism

Longer-Term Preparedness (In Addition to the Basics):

- 1-month supply of food and water
- 1-month supply of prescription medications
- 1-month supply of basic necessities

Over the years, our basic preparedness has been invaluable. During an unusual arctic blast, freezing temperatures caused our pipes to freeze and burst, sending a waterfall through our home. Since this was over Christmas, available plumbers were already overwhelmed, leaving us without water for days. Thankfully, our stored water met our drinking, washing, and basic hygiene needs. Similarly, during the pandemic, our stock of essentials helped us avoid the rush on store supplies and ease demand. Stay prepared—it makes all the difference.

The Relationship Roadmap Top 3 Survey
Partner #1 _____

Movies
1.
2.
3.

Songs
1.
2.
3.

Strengths
1.
2.
3.

TV Shows
1.
2.
3.

Celebrities
1.
2.
3.

Books
1.
2.
3.

Ice Cream Flavors
1.
2.
3.

Vacations
1.
2.
3.

Board/Card Games
1.
2.
3.

Sports to Play
1.
2.
3.

Snacks and Treats
1.
2.
3.

Childhood Toys
1.
2.
3.

Sports to Watch
1.
2.
3.

Cartoons
1.
2.
3.

People You Want to Meet
1.
2.
3.

Musicians
1.
2.
3.

Dates
1.
2.
3.

Meals
1.
2.
3.

The Relationship Roadmap Top 3 Survey
Partner #2 _____

Movies	Songs	Strengths
1.	1.	1.
2.	2.	2.
3.	3.	3.

TV Shows	Celebrities	Books
1.	1.	1.
2.	2.	2.
3.	3.	3.

Ice Cream Flavors	Vacations	Board/Card Games
1.	1.	1.
2.	2.	2.
3.	3.	3.

Sports to Play	Snacks and Treats	Childhood Toys
1.	1.	1.
2.	2.	2.
3.	3.	3.

Sports to Watch	Cartoons	People You Want to Meet
1.	1.	1.
2.	2.	2.
3.	3.	3.

Musicians	Dates	Meals
1.	1.	1.
2.	2.	2.
3.	3.	3.

The Relationship Roadmap 70 Key Ideas and Quotes

These ideas and quotes succinctly capture the message of *The Relationship Roadmap*. May these insights inspire and strengthen your connection.

1. Your happiness is your responsibility, your partner can add joy.

2. Neither partner holds the ultimate blueprint for life—value and blend both perspectives.

3. Revisit dating activities that sparked your connection to reclaim the early relationship magic.

4. Forgiveness doesn't mean forgetting; it's remembering with grace, love, and compassion.

5. Leave mistakes in the past, but carry their lessons forward to shape a better future.

6. You can't change the past, but you design your present. We are the architects of our future.

7. Overwriting past trauma can free you and your partner from negative patterns.

8. Some wounds may never fully heal—and that's okay. Painful memories guide wiser choices.

9. Love your partner by listening intently, noticing nonverbal cues, with genuine interest.

10. In a distracted world, choose to be fully present with your partner.

11. Ask for what you need from your partner when your relationship is thriving.

12. Validate your partner and acknowledge the merit in their opinion, even in disagreement.

13. Letting go of control can lead to the most enjoyable moments in your relationship.

14. Reframe negative thoughts into positive responses to transform your outlook.

15. In relationships, don't give in or give up—give love.

16. An apology followed by "but" becomes an excuse, not a true apology.

17. Apologies are meaningless without changed behavior.

18. Offer and accept forgiveness and grace generously—they are precious gifts.

19. Seeing your partner's perspective is like having a map to avoid misunderstandings.

20. Align with your partner to steer together toward a shared future.

21. Embrace change in your relationship—it's the only constant in life.

22. Family includes those you choose to surround yourself with in deep connection.

23. Match your partner's excitement for their passions, even if just occasionally.

24. Children learn relationship dynamics by observing you, model love and respect.

25. Discuss parenting strategies privately, away from your children.

26. It's okay to say "no" to extra tasks, even if you're a people-pleaser.

27. Keep impressing your partner with your appearance throughout your relationship.

28. Your outward appearance can boost your self-confidence.

29. Strive to be the best version of yourself for you and your partner.

30. Adapt and overcome life's changes to grow stronger together.

31. Prioritizing your partner's happiness can unlock a more fulfilling relationship.

32. Step out of your comfort zone—new experiences can open a wondrous world.

33. Be willing to embrace discomfort for the sake of growth.

34. Put your partner's happiness above your own comfort.

35. Expect the best from shared activities, and your positivity will shape the experience.

36. When nervous about an activity say, "This could be fun!" or better, "This will be fun!"

37. Serving your partner frees up their time, creating space for meaningful connection.

38. Doing what your partner loves shows your love, even if it's not your ideal activity.

39. Make your partner's priorities your own.

40. Boosting your partner's happiness often enhances your own.

41. Cherish traditions, but don't cling to them—change is inevitable.

42. Embrace the "new normal" with an open heart.

43. Join your partner in their hobbies; it's an invitation to their heart.

44. Recognize what you can't change to reduce stress and worry.

45. Limit stress to productive moments—don't let it dominate your life.

46. Healthy living extends your time and quality of life with your partner.

47. Keep your body healthy for your well-being and your shared journey.

48. Believe in your capacity for change and tackling hard things.

49. Living solely for yourself can harm relationships—consider your partner's needs.

50. Celebrate others' success to cultivate joy and peace in your relationship.

51. Be radically happy for those around you.

52. You are not inferior unless you allow yourself to feel that way.

53. Happiness exists only in the present—find it where you are now.

54. Shift "have to" to "get to" for a life filled with gratitude and calm.

55. Laugh at yourself and embrace lighthearted teasing from others.

56. Assume positive intentions behind others' words and actions, even when unclear.

57. Seek opportunities to smile and laugh daily for better mental health.

58. Actively add adventure to your relationship—thinking about it isn't enough.

59. Invest in your financial future for greater flexibility in retirement.

60. Cherish your partner's openness about their desires—it's a map to their heart.

61. Long-term love lets you gaze into your partner's soul with deep, lasting adoration.

62. The grass is greener where you nurture it.

63. Love your partner in ways that resonate most with them.

64. Intentional, purposeful actions are key to loving your partner uniquely.

65. If romance matters to your partner, make it a priority to you.

66. Non-romantic needs are as vital as romance in building a strong bond.

67. Find joy and positivity in every moment of your relationship.

68. Sincere, heartfelt gifts are priceless expressions of love.

69. If your relationship holds hope and goodness, fight for it.

70. Love is a journey—navigate it with intention, care, and joy.

Final Thoughts

I hope the insights and activities in this book enrich your relationship. By completing some of these exercises, you've likely gained a deeper appreciation for what makes your partner unique. Use this newfound understanding to intentionally meet each other's needs.

The challenges in this book are designed to bring you years of joy and connection. We are still enjoying our journey through the Adventure Guide, the 50 States Challenge, and the National Parks Challenges. We invite you to join us in these lifelong, joy-filled pursuits!

No matter where you are in your relationship, there's always room for growth and connection. I'm thrilled for your blossoming love. Embrace adventures, support one another, and let *The Relationship Roadmap* guide your path!

Your friend,
Roger Crooks